Word Bethumped
The Best and Worst of the Wördos

Word Bethumped
The Best and Worst of the Wördos

Jeremiah Reedy & Fred Webber

To order additional copies of this book, contact:
Xlibris
1-888-795-4274
www.Xlibris.com
Orders@Xlibris.com
797593

ABOUT THE AUTHORS

Jeremiah Reedy, a native of South Dakota, earned an S.T.B. degree at the Gregorian University in Rome, an M.A. in Classics from the University of South Dakota, another M.A. and a Ph.D. in Classical Studies from the University of Michigan, where he specialized in classical philology and Indo-European linguistics. He taught Classics at Macalester College in St. Paul, Minnesota, from 1968 until he retired in 2004. For the past 25 years, most of his time and energy have been devoted to studying and writing about Greek philosophy. Besides essays on philosophy, his publications include translations and editions of both ancient Greek and medieval Latin works.. An activist in efforts to reform education, Dr. Reedy was the chair of the founding committee of the New Spirit School in St. Paul and the founder of the Seven Hills Classical Academy in Bloomington, Minnesota.

Coauthor Fred Webber is a native of Minnesota and currently lives in Medina, a suburb of Minneapolis. He and his wife, Sue, live in a senior condominium.

He has a degree in Journalism from the University of Minnesota.

Virtually all of his career was spent working for advertising agencies, where he learned a great deal about writing but never was a writer. He was blessed too with gifted writers and art directors.

For many years he has been a member of the Wördos, a group of people interested in the use of words, especially in mass media.

Fred is a part-time copyeditor for Outdoor News Publications in Plymouth, Minnesota.

This is his first "half" book.

CHAPTER I
Who are the Wördos?

Wördos are people who care about the precise and accurate use of the English language. We want to be sure there is CLARITY in communication. We believe that the failure to write clearly jeopardizes understanding and believability and that writing well is important in establishing credibility and competence.

The group was founded in the early 1980s. One of the founders was Björn Björnson. It is in his memory that we use the umlaut in Wördos.

Björnson, in an essay published in 1972, clearly set the tone for our group and defined its purpose with these memorable words:

> "I plead with you to use your mother tongue properly. Every misuse of a word debases it, as well as clouds the thought you wish to convey. Every ignorant addition to the language lowers its standards and lessens its value. Words are a medium by which ideas are exchanged. Don't inflate our language and rob it of its intrinsic worth. The English language is a precious heritage. It is a rich tongue derived from many sources and is capable of expressing every nuance of thought and feeling. Cherish your linguistic heritage and pass it on in undiminished vigor to future generations."

Our goal is to translate Björn Björnson's idealism into reality.

We meet the third Wednesday of every month to talk about words. (No surprise there.) Some of us are retired senior newspaper executives. Some are current or former writers, editors, or teachers. Some of us, heaven forbid, are former advertising people. All of us are interested in words, their meanings and their usage. At our meetings we discuss the errors we have found in all media, primarily local, but any source is a good source.

A few years ago we published a book, "92 abuses of English that drive curmudgeons crazy!" The fifth edition of the book was published in 2004. "Copies are for sale. Cheap"

We do have some rules. This first one is: we have no rules. We have no chairman, president, or officers of any kind. We have no articles of incorporation or bylaws. We have no dues, no minutes, and no social chairman. We have no members. (We do have interested people who show up for meetings. They are "attendees.") We do not discuss our health or grandchildren.

According to a Star Tribune article covering one of our meetings, "Wördos are local self-proclaimed guardians of the printed and broadcast word. For two hours Wednesday they discussed grammar and spelling mistakes, the New York Times scandal, reading about a 'bargain basement upstairs' and a sign that said, 'We can repair anything. Knock hard. Bell doesn't work.'"

Probably the best description is that we are a group of people who enjoy the language and try to protect it for others.

We read newspapers - local and national - magazines, signs in restrooms ("please wash hands for the person after you,"), just about anything printed, and listen to radio and watch TV. Broadcast media seem to be especially fertile ground for Wördos.

We aren't pedantic and we're not elitists. We enjoy the humorous use, or misuse, of our language, respect its intention and rules, and try to save as much of it as possible.

Watch Your Language, or The Wördos will Get You

By Mary Divine
St. Paul Pioneer Press
Posted: 06/28/2013

Wördos member Marlene Reuber from St. Paul reads from a local newspaper as the group met to talk about words at their monthly meeting at Friendship Village in Bloomington. (Pioneer Press: John Doman)

Whenever a group of 15 retired reporters, editors, writers and teachers get together to discuss the English language, a subject dear to their hearts, talk inevitably turns to the Oxford comma.

Chuck Sweningsen, 87, of Bloomington said he had wrestled with the Oxford comma (aka serial comma) — a comma before the word "and" or "or" at the end of a list — while editing a newsletter.

"How do you punctuate words that are in a series?" he asked the group. "Do you put a comma before the last 'and,' or don't you?"

Most of the men and women — who call themselves "The Wördos" — are retired from careers in which they spent, collectively, 450 years in the daily writing, editing and proofreading of the English language.

The group advocates clear and accurate writing and cares about things such as the Oxford comma; most of the group, by the way, favor its use.

Read more:
https://www.twincities.com/2013/06/27/watch-your-language-or-the-Wördos-will-get-you/

FYI

The Wördos meet at 10 a.m. on the third Wednesday of each month at Friendship Village in Bloomington. The meetings are open to the public. For more information, contact Fred Webber at phred55427@ aol.com or 763-545-4582.

CHAPTER II
How I Got Hooked on Words

Jeremiah Reedy

I am wordstruck,
word bethumped
word besotted, wordaholic,
unrepentant verbivore.
Richard Lederer

In a wonderful column that appeared some years ago in the *Saturday Review* the poet John Ciardi related a number of experiences he had while teaching composition after World War II. Among his students was a navy veteran who had served aboard a tanker that refueled ships at sea and whose ambition was to become a writer. In a story about his war experiences this veteran wrote, "We had arrived at our mid-ocean rendezvous." In a conference Ciardi pointed out that "arrive" comes, via French, from Latin *ripa,* "bank," "shore" *(cf.* riparian and riviera) and that the student had said in effect, "We had come to shore in mid-ocean." Did he want to say that?" Everyone knows that "to arrive" means 'to get there' and who cares about dead Latin roots?" was his response. That student never published a thing, according to Ciardi, because he lacked the desire to engage language at a depth beyond the superficial, a desire that a good writer must have. The same student saw nothing unusual about the phrase "a crusading Egyptian social worker" even after Ciardi pointed out the derivation of crusade (Latin *crux,* "cross") and the fact that "Egyptians were not generally motivated in that direction, that they tended, in fact, to be on the other side of those expeditions we call the crusades ..." I believe it was Ciardi who, on another occasion, objected to the phrase "a delapidated wooden shack" on the grounds that stones (*lapides* in Latin) don't fall off wooden shacks. He likewise found fault with "supercilious wave of the hand" because it involved a comic confusion of anatomy (*supercilium* is Latin for eyebrow). I heard Ciardi speak once in St. Paul, and he confessed that he was a "compulsive etymologizer." He was the first person I had met who suffered from the same strange affliction I suffered from for about thirty years, i.e. a compulsion to trace the etymology of every word I encountered. I came to feel that I didn't really know a word unless I knew its origin—Latin, Greek, Anglo-Saxon, or whatever and better yet its Proto-Indo-European root. I hope readers will discover, as I did, that this is actually a blessing and the source of many insights and much joy. In my case this fascination with the origins of words seems to have begun with two courses I was asked to teach at the U. of South Dakota—"Scientific Terminology" and "Derivatives." In this chapter I want to share with readers some of the fruits of my passion for etymology and perhaps even engender it in others.

A friend attended a seminar on "thanatology" (on death and dying). She said they discussed death as a "viable alternative!" Besides using a dreadful cliche, she had come close to saying that death is a live option since viable comes through French *vie* from Latin *vita* and means "capable of living." Had it been deliberate, I might have been impressed by her use of oxymoron. I am reminded of the police chief who called charges of graft in his department "potentially factual" and of the corporation executive who said that the accident at Three Mile Island was a "normal aberration."

W. H. Auden, another poet, was once asked what advice he would give an aspiring poet. Auden said he would ask why the person wanted to write. "If the answer was 'Because I have something terribly important to say'... there could be small hope of expecting poetry from him. If, on the other hand, the answer was 'Because I like to hang around words and overhear them whisper to one another,' then that man might fail of any of thousands of human reasons, but he had a poet's interest in the poem and could be hoped for."

A by-product of the study of Latin and a goal of the study of "derivatives" should be not only a numerical increase in the size of the students' vocabularies, but the enhancement of their ability to appreciate the deeper levels of meanings words have. I always tried to make my students philologists in the etymological sense of the word (lovers of words and language) and share with them the joy that comes from "hanging around words." Now, there may be people who have developed a love for words and an appreciation for their histories and connotations without studying Latin, but they are indeed *rarae aves*. Clearly the study of Latin is the best way to become a connoisseur of words, and clearly vocabulary building courses are "second best." Nevertheless, given the difficulty (often impossibility) of requiring or persuading students to take Latin, courses that deal with roots, prefixes, suffixes, word-formation, etymology, etc., suddenly seem very important.

Charles Ferguson, senior editor emeritus of *Reader's Digest*, novelist, biographer *(Naked to Mine Enemies)*, essayist, lecturer, historian *(Organizing to Beat The Devil*, a history of the Methodist Church), teacher *(Say It with Words)* and logophile extrordinaire used to visit Macalester every year, and we became friends. He once wrote in a letter to me that a word "should be treated as an entity, as an Emersonian person so real it will bleed, as a world that sums up eons of life, as a thing in itself, not a blob on a page or a noise in the ear. A word is to be seen as history marvelously compressed, as a distillate of human experience because it has had human experience passing in and out of minds and across tongues in countless situations, witnessing and savoring what has gone on in *its* presence and by means of it." Mr. Ferguson reminds us of Samuel Coleridge's statement that "there are cases in which more knowledge of more value may be expressed by the history of a word than by the history of a campaign." Thanks to the generosity of "Fergy," as we called him, Macalester had for a number of years a "Word Library," a special room in the library with a collection of dictionaries, lexicons, and books about words, of which there is a surprising number. It was Fergy's ambition to make it "the best known and most used bank of word data in the world" and to make Macalester a center for the study of words (not of linguistics or semantics or of any —ology, but of plain old words." After Mr. Ferguson's death and the construction of the new library, the "Word Library" unfortunately ceased to exist.

Words come with retinues of associations and connotations. They have textures, shapes, tastes and histories. Words have their particular demands upon the speech muscles. According to George Steiner words have "angularities," "concavities," "forces of tectonic suggestion," and "rugosity" (wrinkles); for poets words even have distinctive smells. Homer speaks of "wooly" screams, Dante of "hairy" and "shaggy'" words, also "combed out," "glossy," and "rumpled" ones.

> Pablo Neruda, the Chilean writer, says, "Words have shadow, transparence, weight, feathers, hair, and everything gathered from so much wandering from country to country, from being roots so long ... Words are very ancient and very new...." And again "I run after certain words ... they are so beautiful that I want to fit them all into my poem ... I catch them in midflight, as they buzz past, I trap them, clean them, peel them, I set myself in front of the dish, they have a crystalline texture to me, vibrant, ivory, vegetable, oily, like fruit, like algae, like agates, like olives. And then I stir them, I shake them, I drink them, I gulp them down, I mash them, I garnish them, I let them go ... I leave them in my poem like stalactites, like slivers of polished wood, like coals, pickings from a shipwreck, gifts from the waves ... Everything exists in the word."

Beside poets no one is more sensitive to these dimensions of language today than Madison Avenue. "There are tall, skinny words and short, fat ones, and strong ones and weak ones, and boy words and girl words," writes an advertising agency. Fire, passion, explode, smash and attack are described as red words. Moss, brook, cool, solitude and hammock are examples of green words. There are also black words (funeral, tomb, somber) and beige ones (abstruse, clerk, and float).

"Shout is red, persuade is green, rave is black and listen is beige." Young words are pancake, bat, ball and surprise; old ones, Packard, lavender and velvet. "Confident, smug words" are proud, stare, dare and major; ulcer, itch and stomach are worried words. "Joe is confident; Horace is worried." Some words are round, some oblong, some are shaped like Rorschach ink blots, some are square. There are fast words and slow words too. "Wilkinsburg, as you would expect, is dry, square, old and light gray." Truly, as Emerson said, "language is fossil poetry."

Words can be important source of insight, and there have been philosophers who showed great interest in the ancient wisdom enshrined in them. William Barrett says this about the German philosopher Heidegger: "The etymologies of words, particularly Greek words are a passion with Heidegger; in his pursuit of them he has been accused of playing with words, but when one realizes what deposits of truth mankind has let slip into its language as it evolves, Heidegger's perpetual digging at words to get at their hidden nuggets of meaning is one of his most exciting facets. In the matter of Greek particularly—a dead language whose whole history is now spread out before us— we can see how certain truths are embedded in the language itself; truths that the Greek race later came to *forget* in its thinking. The word 'phenomenon'—a word in ordinary usage, by this time, in all modern European languages—means in Greek 'that which reveals itself.' Phenomenology therefore means for Heidegger the attempt to let the thing speak for itself. Heidegger finds around that word a whole cluster of etymologies, all of them having an internal unity of meaning that brings us to the very center of his thought. The etymology of the Greek word for truth, *aletheia*, is another key to Heidegger's theory: the word means literally, "unhiddenness," "revelation." Truth occurs when what has been hidden is no longer so." Finally, "It is by harking back to the primeval meaning of truth as it became embedded in the Greek language that Heidegger takes his theory in a single leap beyond the boundaries of Husserl's phenomenology."

William James in a chapter on mysticism in *Varieties of Religious Experience* discusses the insights that individual words or phrases can produce. These insights are the "simplest rudiment of mystical experience. They lie at one extreme of a continuum, the end that usually makes no claims regarding supernatural origin or content. An author named John Foster testified that "single words (as *chalcedony)*, or the names of ancient heroes, had a mighty fascination over him. 'At any time the word hermit was enough to transport him.' The words *woods* and *forest* would produce the most powerful emotion." A German lady confessed to James that "Philadelphia" had haunted her all her life, and she longed to visit the city that had such a wondrous name. Martin Luther one day when be heard a fellow monk recite the words from the creed, "I believe in the forgiveness of sins" says he suddenly saw the scriptures in a new light; he felt as if he had been born again. It was as if "I had found the door of Paradise thrown wide open."

It is well known that the name *Oedipus* can mean etymologically "know foot" and "swell-foot." John Hay, author of a recent book on *Oedipus the King,* believes that the "catalytic insight," the "epiphany" (defined as "the sudden realization of the *whatness* of a thing") that made the greatest of tragedies possible came to Sophocles as he contemplated the possible meanings of Oedipus' name. Sophocles did not take one meaning and reject the other; he considered both meanings simultaneously and saw that lameness was an apt metaphor for human knowledge. Human knowing is like the journey of a lame man! Sophocles calls the audience's attention to this insight by means of etymological wordplay, which, Hay says, is a "major source of insight and irony. It goes back to the root-meanings of the word for a fresh or 'reborn' slant."

Margaret Schlauch has an admirable discussion of the etymological use of words by poets in Chapter 9 of *The Gift of Language* where she gives a number of excellent examples. Her conclusion: "Sophisticated writers still impose the etymological task upon their readers as part of the aesthetic experience. It may be said, in fact, that etymology is one of the devices by which readers are now called upon to share in the creative act."

The remainder of this chapter provides examples of curiosities and oddities and even some non-trivial matters which readers may find of interest. I used to use these for three or four minutes at the beginning of classes to capture the students' attention and to inject a bit of levity into the learning process. Also, when Macalester had a one-month January term, I taught a course called "Philology for Logophiles" a couple of times which was designed to interest students in Latin, Greek, and linguistics. A whole course in "recreational linguistics" was offered at the University of Massachusetts, Amherst, which dealt exclusively with word games, puzzles, euphemisms, limericks, double dactyls, macaronic verse, word squares, etc.

The literary avant-garde: There used to be in Paris a group of writers and intellectuals who call themselves "Oulipo," short for *Ouvroir de Letterature Potentielle* ("Workshop of Potential Literature"). They met monthly to discuss experimental forms. An American member invented "perverbs" (perverted proverbs), *e.g.* "Think twice before speaking to a friend in need." Another member composed the longest known palindrome, a 5,000 word treatise on palindromes. Another composed *Cent Mille Milliards de Poems (A Hundred Thousand Billion Poems).* The reader can construct 10^{14} intelligible sonnets by flipping strips of paper each of which contains one verse. Other fruits of their labors include Spoonerisms, poems on Mobius strips and emblematic poems (poems shaped like pyramids, hearts, bottles, etc.).

Lipograms are compositions that leave out one letter of the alphabet. Georges Perec, a contemporary French novelist, for instance, wrote a "highly praised novel," *La Disparition,* in which there is not a single e. (Some critics didn't notice the omission!) Ernest V. Wright likewise used no e's in his 50,000 word novel *Gadsby;* he tied the E type-bar down in his typewriter. (For a discussion of the difficulties involved in such an effort see Martin Gardiner's note in *Oddities and Curiosities of Words and Literature* by C. Bombaugh. Gardiner does not, unfortunately, tell us why people write lipograms.) Pindar, the ancient Greek poet, according to Athenaeus, wrote an ode without sigmas, and according to Addison (#50 of the *Spectator)* one Tryphiodorus wrote an *Odyssey* in 24 books ostracizing alpha from the first book, beta from the second, etc.

At the other end of the spectrum, a monk named Hucbald used only words beginning with c in his *Ecloga de Laudibus Calvitti (Carmina clarisonae calvis cantate Camenae/ comere condigno conabor carmine caivas. etc.)* There is also the *Pugna Porcorum* by Petrus Placentius in which every word begins with, guess what.

Palindromes: (Spelled the same forwards and backwards) "Eva, can I pose as Aesop in a cave?" "Red rum, sir, is murder." There are hundreds more of these in Howard W. Bergerson's *Palindromes and Anagrams;* Bombaugh also has a short chapter on palindromes which includes several in Latin and Greek (Lawyer's motto: Si *nummi, immunis.* "If you have money, you're immune.") According to an article in the N.Y. Times, *Roma, summus amor* was found among the graffiti on the walls of a tavern recently by archaeologists excavating under *Santa Maria Maggiore* in Rome. If one wants more palindromes, see "Manner of Speaking" by J. Ciardi for more examples and further bibliography or contact Professor Otto R. Osseforp, c/o *The Wall Street Journal.*

Centos (Latin, "a garment made of rags sewed together, a patchwork") are poems that consist of lines and phrases taken from other poems; they are also called "mosaic poems." The *Cento Nuptialis* of Ausonius is perhaps the most famous example. The Empress Eudoxia wrote a life of Christ using lines and parts of lines from Homer, and Proba Falconia and Alexander Ross *(fl. 1769)* did the same using Vergil. There are modern examples in Bombaugh.

Anagrams (=Ars Magna) a "frivolous and now almost obsolete intellectual exercise" according to Bombaugh. The letters of the first line should be rearranged to form a second line which must say something relevant to the first, *e.g.* James Stuart—A just master. Imperators/A prime sort. Senator/A Nestor. Sinecure/Sure nice! *Supremus Pontifex Romanus/O non sum super petram fixus.* United States/*In te Deus stat.*

Neologisms: Gelett Burgess once wrote a dictionary containing several hundred words he had coined, entitled *Burgess Unabridged. A Dictionary of Words You Have Always Needed.* As far as I know only two of his coinages have made it into other dictionaries, "goop" and "blurb." Other examples: "Lallifaction, n. A verbose story, a joke repeated" and "Huzzlecoo, n. 1. An intimate talk; a 'heart-to-heart talk,' a conversation. 2. A flirtation." The editor of the *National Observer* coined some new words and was deluged with readers' own inventions. Among the better ones: "Xerocracy, government by photocopy." "Idiolectuals, overschooled and undereducated nitwits who have solutions for all problems." and "Msdemeanor, any offense against women's liberation." "Factoid" was coined by Norman Mailer. Coining words would be a good exercise for students and could even teach them something about word formation. One might start with new names for groups a la "pride of lions," "parliament of owls," and "nide of pheasants," *e.g* a "declension of Latin teachers."

Improper nouns: What do silhouette, zeppelin, raglan, cardigan, leotard, tawdry and dunce have in common? The same thing that ocean, pamphlet, joviality, martial and kewpie share—they were once all proper nouns, i.e. people's names. There are eighty-two of these in *Word People* by Nancy Sorel and hundreds, perhaps thousands, in Willard Espy's *Thou Improper, Thou Uncommon Noun.*

Rare words: Mrs. Byrne's *Dictionary of Unusual, Obscure and Preposterous Words* is guaranteed to provide hours of enjoyment for logophiles. There one learns what a *fossarian* is, also what *clinomania* is and what *luctiferous, apopemploclinic; cinerescent* and *retromingent* mean. *Poplollies and Bellibones* have more of the same: *blore, faffle, iswonk, keak, quop* and *snollygoster* are examples. Students are amused by words such as *nosarian* (one who believes that there is no limit to the possible size of noses). They should, however, be warned not to waste time learning them, although such "nonce words" could be used to test students' knowledge of constituent elements.

More Perverbs: "When in Rome, do it yourself." "Two heads is better than none." "Don't count your chickens in midstream." "No news is the mother of invention." "A fool and his money is a friend indeed."

Redundancies: Rules and regulations, due and payable, hoot and holler, leaps and bounds, neat and tidy, vim and vigor, tattered and torn, plain and simple, rant and rave, aches and pains, cease and desist, null and void, over and above, lord and master, each and every, prim and proper, safe and sound, and there are many more. Some of these are legal phrases.

Malaproprisms: "She has really plummeted to the top." "He's going up and down like a metronome." "Republicans understand the importance of bondage between a mother and child." (Dan Quayle)

"Well, that was a cliff-dweller." (Re a close game.) "We seem to have unleased a hornet's nest." "He's as headstrong as an allegory on the banks of the Nile." (Mrs. Malaprop herself).

Aptonyms: (a hideous hybrid word since "apt-" is Latin and "–onym" is Greek, but you'll get the idea.) Cardinal Sin was the head of the Catholic Church in the Philippines. Mr. Sues is a lawyer. Miss Cashdollar was the treasurer of a school. Linda Toot played the flute in the Milwaukee Symphony. John Wisdom is an American philosopher. Dr. Richard Bone is an osteopath. A guy named Hooker runs a bait shop. Dr. I. Doctor, Eye Doctor, is an ophthalmologist. There's a used car dealer named Karl Krook. Jared Wooley raises sheep. Dr. Hertz was a dentist in Ft. Lauderdale, Dr. Slaughter is an oral surgeon, Dr. Coffin, M.D. is a general practitioner! and Rev. D. Goodenough is a Methodist minister.

Linguicide: "Did I hear you say 'hopefullywise'?" (cartoon) "Dvorak was a late bloomer compositionwise." (Program notes) "She was as pure as a vestigial virgin:' (student paper) "He was a life long native of N. Y." (N. Y. Times). "We must tentify these conclusions." (bureaucrat) "Young juveniles" (mayor of Boston) "a false lie" (Billy Martin) "free gifts" (bank: ad), focalize, prioritize, youthfulize, deniability and on and on. Pomposity, redundancy, evasiveness, ambiguity, obfuscation, jargon and psychobabble everywhere, but the question is, "Is it serious?" Yes, according to Richard Mitchell, "The Undergound Grammarian, who makes a very strong case for traditional ideas about grammar and composition in *Less Than Words Can Say.* The classic discussion of this subject, however, is George Orwell's essay, "Politics and the English Language." He thought it was a serious matter: "But if thought corrupts language, language can also corrupt thought." According to Sydney J. Harris, the columnist, "If the level of verbal expression is low, the only other form of expression is physical." In other words, those who are unable to express themselves verbally are more likely to resort to the fist (or a gun) than those who are articulate. Without an adequate vocabulary "such abstract ideas as justice, honesty, personal property, law, courtesy and thoughtfulness for others seem impossible to comprehend."

In 2004 I read an article by a high school English teacher in a local publication in which she explained that most public schools no longer teach grammar explicitly, only implicitly. I took this to mean that they don't teach it at all, which in many cases is true. She explained that teaching grammar would take time away from teaching more valuable "higher order thinking skills" such as analysis, synthesis, critical thinking and even "metacognitive strategies" (thinking about one's thinking). This article provoked me to write an op-ed piece in which I complained that many students come to college not knowing the parts of speech or even how to pick out the subject and predicate in a sentence. I told a story about coming to a chapter on participles in an elementary Latin class. I asked if anyone knew what a participle was. After a long silence a young lady said, "They are not supposed to dangle." That was the sum total of the class's knowledge of participles. She didn't know what a participle was, but she had heard that they are not supposed to dangle. I then argued in my essay that it is absurd to think that students who can't analyze a sentence will be able to analyze an argument, an editorial, or a campaign speech. *The Pioneer Press* published my piece under the title "Our Participles are Dangling and We Don't Even Know It."

A short time later the *Wall Street Journal* ran a story in which the author claimed that the public schools were doing a poor job of teaching grammar. I revised my *Pioneer Press* essay somewhat and send it to the *Journal* which published it under the title "Us Don't Need Grammar for Higher Order Thinking Skills." As a result of these efforts, I received a phone call from a gentleman who was the president of a group called the "Wördos." He wanted to come to my office to talk with me about grammar and related subjects, and, of course, I invited him to come. The Wördos are retired editors, reporters and writers who meet once a month to discuss words and grammar and language in general. Between meetings, as they read newspapers, listen to the radio, watch TV, etc., they scrutinize everything for grammatical errors, stylistic infelicities, neologisms, and other linguistic matters of interest. These are discussed at the monthly meetings, after which the president puts out a newsletter which is sent to 350 newspapers in Minnesota. When I asked what sort of replies he receives, he replied, "The silence is thunderous." The Wördos invited me to speak at their next meeting which I did, and then they invited me to join, which I also did.

At seventy I was one of the youngest members. Most are in their 80s; one resigned shortly after I joined explaining that he would soon celebrate his 90th birthday. At our meetings we have a hilarious time, and I look forward eagerly to each session. Following the format used in earlier parts of this chapter, I will share with readers some of the gems garnered at meetings of the Wördos.

Amusing headlines: "One-armed man applauds the kindness of strangers," "Statistics show that teen pregnancy drops off significantly after age 25," "Attorney accidentally sues himself," "County to pay $250,000 to advertise lack of funds," "Tiger Woods plays with own balls, Nike says," "Federal Agents Raid Gun Shop, Find Weapons," "Fish need water, Feds say." "Community rallies to help massacre survivors." "University of Akron students protest invasion by Israel." "Lawmaker questions prison costs of killing suspect." "A religious mother questions her beliefs after her gay son kills himself and eventually joins the crusade for gay rights." Coupon: "Get 50% off or half price, whichever is less."

Why English is not easy: "The farm used to produce produce." "We must polish the Polish furniture." "He could lead if he would get the lead out." "The soldier decided to desert his dessert in the desert." "Since there is no time like the present, he thought it was time to present the present." "When shot at, the dove dove into the bushes." "The buck does funny things when the does are present." "To help with planting, the farmer taught his sow to sow." "The wind was too strong to wind the sail." Note the following: "There is no egg in eggplant, nor ham in hamburger; neither apple nor pine in pineapple. French fries weren't invented in France. Sweetmeats are candies while sweetbreads, which aren't sweet, are meat. Quicksand works slowly, boxing rings are square, and a guinea pig is neither from Guinea nor is it a pig."

Things that make Wördos [sic]: Using "less" where "fewer" is called for (e.g. in supermarket, "Ten items or less." "Between you and I." "Myself" as subject ("Myself and my wife are going to the movie.") "Who" used instead of "whom." (This is a lost cause; "whom" is doomed.) Using "like" instead of "as." Using the plural pronoun to refer to one person: "Each student should bring their book." Using an adjective where an adverb is called for: "She learns very quick." Using the indicative in a contrary-to-fact condition: "If it was raining, I would be unhappy." (Should be "If it were raining...") Not using the possessive before a gerund (a word ending in -ing used as a noun): "Aside from him being an athlete..." "If you don't mind me asking..." "Us working together is very important..." (Obama) "Thusly" for "Thus" ("Thus" is an adverb and doesn't need the "–ly.") "Hopefully" (The dog went home hopefully.) "Alright" is not all right. Confusion between "lie" and "lay" (Another lost cause, I fear.)

I conclude with this quote from a review of John Moore's *You English Words:* "If a man must go soppy about something––and no doubt a man must––what better object could there be for his daft, uncritical, wife-maddening, friend-alienating affection than the English language?" (*Time,* August, 1962).

CHAPTER III
How the World's Worst Teacher Changed My Life

In 1961 I was a graduate student at the University of Michigan. During the summer there was a course listed in the summer session catalogue entitled "Comparative Grammar of Latin and Greek" to be taught by a visiting professor from Yale named Warren Cowgill (1929-1985). The first day of class there were *ca.* twenty-eight enrolled—twenty five high school Latin teachers and three graduate students, myself and two others. Cowgill, who was the most eccentric person I had ever encountered, entered the room, shuffled to the desk, sat on the edge of his chair, looked at the sidewall, mumbled a few words no one could understand, and then proceeded to fill the side blackboard plus the front one, and the other side one with paradigms of nouns and verbs in a language none of us knew—it was most likely Hittite, one of his specialties. This took the whole period, and, as we filed out, I heard some of the Latin teachers say they were going to drop. The second day of class the same thing happened, the paradigms may have been in Sanskrit or Tocharian (once spoken in Northwest China), and more Latin teachers dropped. The third day was identical—more mumbling and more paradigms in an exotic language none of us knew, and the last of the Latin teachers dropped. Later that day, we three grad students went to see him during his office hours. We reminded him that we were students of Latin and Greek and that his course was entitled "Comparative Grammar of Latin and Greek." We told him we didn't know what was going on in class. He was surprised—he thought we were "right with it." We explained that we didn't know the exotic languages he was dealing with. He promised he would take up Greek the following day.

The next day his method was the same, but as he put paradigms of Greek nouns and verbs on the board, he pointed out similarities with Latin, and occasionally he mentioned Sanskrit and German and even English. Suddenly, a light bulb went on in my head. I had been studying Latin and Greek as if they were almost totally unrelated, and I had been using vocabulary cards to memorize Greek vocabulary items by rote memory not noticing in many cases that there were cognates in Latin, German, and English. Cowgill's class turned out to be not only comparative grammar of Latin and Greek, but an introduction to Indo-European linguistics. I found Proto-Indo-European roots absolutely fascinating, and this is how the world's worst teacher changed my life. Cardinal Newman is reported to have said, "The teacher's main duty is to inspire." Cowgill clearly inspired me and no doubt countless others later. Looking at his teaching in this way, one would have to call him an excellent teacher.

Cowgill went on to become "one of the 20th century's greatest linguists... [his] dazzling mastery of the entire Indo-European linguistic world is on full display, with every work a model of expert methodology and depth of thinking"[1] writes the editor of his collected works.

The following semester I took Sanskrit which, together with the interest in Proto-Indo-European I gained from Cowgill, made me a "closet" etymologist. I came to feel that I didn't know a word unless I knew its etymology. I say "closet" etymologist because I considered etymology a "gee whiz" sort of thing, something I should keep to myself, not really a serious scholarly endeavor.

In 1969 the first edition of the *American Heritage Dictionary* (AHD hereafter)[2] appeared with its wonderful article "Indo-European and I-E Roots." (The latest edition also has an article on "Proto-Semitic Language and Culture" and a dictionary of Semitic Roots. Prior to the publication of the AHD one had to know German to access information regarding these roots.) By this time I had realized what an exciting, useful, fascinating, and profound field etymology is, being as it is a part of historical linguistics.

I can thank the German philosopher Martin Heidegger for a second "aha moment." Heidegger thought that by studying the etymology of Greek philosophical terms he could recover their original and true meaning. He compared doing etymology to doing archaeology in that both fields involve "excavating" ancient things to discover valuable and possibly informative and beautiful "things."[3] William Barrett in his book *Irrational Man* says this about Heidegger:

> The etymologies of words, particularly Greek words are a passion with Heidegger; in his pursuit of them he has been accused of playing with words, but when one realizes what deposits of truth mankind has let slip into its language as it evolves, Heidegger's perpetual digging at words to get a their hidden nuggets of meanings is one of his most exciting facets. In the matter of Greek particularly—a dead language whose whole history is now spread out before us—we can see how certain truths are embedded in the language itself; truths that the Greek race later came to forget in its thinking. The word 'phenomenon'—a word in ordinary usage, by this time, in all modern European languages—means in Greek 'that which reveals itself.' Phenomenology, therefore, means for Heidegger the attempt to let the thing speak for itself. Heidegger finds around the word a whole cluster of etymologies, all of them having an internal unity of meaning that brings us to the very center of his thought. The etymology of the Greek word for truth, *aletheia*, is another key to Heidegger's theory: the word means literally, "unhiddenness," "revelation." Truth occurs when what has been hidden is no longer so." Finally, "It is by harking back to the primeval meaning of truth as it became embedded in the Greek language that Heidegger takes his theory in a single leap beyond the boundaries of Husserl's phenomenology."[4]

The thought occurred to me that it might be interesting and even fruitful to examine the etymology of theological terms, as Heidegger examined philosophical terms, to see if there might be bits of ancient wisdom to be found there. Hence, I read through *A Concise Dictionary of Theology* by Gerald O'Collins, S.J. and Edward Farrugia[5] which I chose almost at random from the library shelves. I looked specifically for words whose current meaning is different from their etymological meaning.

One of the first words to attract my attention was prophet. If one were to ask people today what prophets do, almost everyone would say, "they predict the future." In Greek, however, *pro-* did not mean what *pre*-means in Latin as in "predict." The *AHD* gives four meanings for pro- "acting in the place of another" and "supporting, favoring as in prorevolutionary" and pro- meaning "earlier as in procambium," and "in front of, as in procephalic."[6] Greek and Roman prophets did not predict the future; they tried to ascertain the will of the gods, e.g. by observing the flight of birds. According to the *Oxford Classical Dictionary* an ancient prophet was one "who spoke for or in the name of a god or interpreted his or her will."[7]

An online source[8] says that seeing the future was something Hebrew prophets could do, but they were far more than just a person with that ability.

> A prophet is basically a spokesman for G-d, a person chosen by G-d to speak to people on G-d's behalf and convey a message or teaching. Prophets were role models of holiness, scholarship and closeness to G-d. They set standards for the entire community. The Hebrew word for a prophet, *navi* (*Nun-Beit-Yod-Alef*) comes from the term *niv sefatayim* meaning 'fruit of the lips' which emphasizes the prophet's role as a speaker."

Prophet is then the kind of word I was and am looking for—one whose contemporary meaning is different from the meaning it had in antiquity when it was coined.

It is worth noting here that it has been argued that the ancient Greeks and Romans were not "future oriented." Greek mythology taught that the Golden Age had come first, and then the Silver Age. In other words, the human condition was deteriorating. Our being "future-oriented" and our belief in progress comes from the Judeo-Christian tradition.[9]

If one asked people today what hermits do, nearly everyone would say, "Hermits are people who live alone." Hermit, however, is from the Greek word for "desert," and ancient hermits didn't necessarily live alone. When St. Jerome decided to move from Rome to the Syrian desert, he took his library, two scribes, and a young Jewish convert who tutored him in Hebrew. They all lived together in a cave. (The reason for the scribes was because in antiquity, if someone had a book you wanted, you would borrow it from him and have your scribe make a copy for you.) There were numerous hermits living in the Syrian desert. They seemed to interact constantly. Since Jerome had been an important person in Rome, many friends came to visit him, and important people came from Antioch to consult with him. It is not clear how long Jerome lived in the desert (one year? two years? longer?), but eventually the Syrian hermits grew jealous of him and drove him out. The important point here, nevertheless, is that most hermits living in the dessert were not living solitary lives.[10]

The *AHD* defines auspices as "observation and divination from the action of birds." The au- is the base of Latin *avis*, bird and -spic- is from the root *spec-* "to observe." Romulus and Remus were twins, and when they became old enough to rule, there was a dispute as to where their new city should be located and which of the two should be the king. Romulus favored the Palatine Hill, but Remus preferred the Aventine Hill. To settle the dispute they decided to consult the birds. Each stood on his respective hill with his followers. Soon Remus claimed to have seen six birds while a few minutes later Romulus said he saw twelve. Remus claimed to be the winner by priority; Romulus by number. There are different versions regarding what happened next, but all agree on the outcome: Romulus killed Remus and became the first king of Rome.

The Latin word for prophet is *vates, -is*. There is a rare English word "vatic" which means "pertaining to a prophet." The related Latin verb which means "to prophesy" is *vaticinor, vaticinari,* which doesn't reveal the etymology immediately. The related adjective *vaticanus,* however, does; *vaticinor* comes from *vates* and *cano, -ere* "to sing." The Vatican Hill must have been one of the places to which Roman prophets went to observe the birds and chant their prophesies. *Templum* originally meant "a section, a part cut off" (from the P.I.E. *tem-, *tom- *tm- "cut"). Prophets marked off ("cut off") a space, a *templum* (the -p- is "excrescent"), in which they stood to watch the birds which were bringing messages from the gods. Long before St. Peter was martyred on the Vatican Hill, it had been a sacred place with its own *templum*.

Our word bishop comes from Greek *episcopos* ("overseer"). (In medieval Latin the form *biscopus* occurs.) There is, however, another word for bishop in Latin, *viz. antistes* which provides us with something amusing. The original form of this word was **antestes* which means etymologically "the one who stands ahead" meaning, I assume, the one who stood up front at meetings. However, because of "vowel weakening" **antestes* became *antistes* which, since *anti-* in Greek means "against," a wag might say that the bishop is one who "stands against him."[11]

Hermeneutics is the science or art of interpreting texts, especially sacred ones. Follett's *The Classic Greek Dictionary* relates this word to Hermes, who is defined by the AHD as "the [Greek] god of commerce, invention, cunning, and a thief who also served as messenger, scribe, and herald for the other gods." Christian and Jewish scripture scholars may be surprised to learn that the name of their specialty hermeneutics may come from the name of a pagan god which is bad enough, but he was also a thief!

Sacerdos, the Latin word for priest, derives from P.I.E. **sak-ro-dhot,"* one who performs sacred rites." "Priest" is usually explained as coming from Greek *presbuteros,* the comparative of *presbus,* an old man, an elder which is itself a comparative.

Agape is the word used by Jesus for "love." Its derivation is unknown; hence it had no undesirable connotations whereas the other two candidates did. *Eros* had erotic connotations which made it unsuitable for the love between God and humans, and *philia* meant "friendship" making it also unsuitable.

Some random thoughts: Enthusiasm comes from Greek *entheos* and means etymologically "having a god within." The Sanhedrin was "the ancient Jewish court system," and the Great Sanhedrin was the "supreme religious body in the land of Israel..."[12] The word is derived from Greek *syn-* "with, together" and *hedra,* "seat." It is surprising that the name of the supreme Jewish court comes from Greek. Also, given the changes in the word, it must have been borrowed quite early.

This article was a first humble attempt to identify what can be learned from the etymology of theological terms.

NOTES

1   *The Collected Writings of Warren Cowgill* edited by Jared Klein. "This volume contains all the published articles and reviews, plus a selection of previously unpublished material, by one of the 20th century's greatest linguists, the late Yale University professor Warren Cowgill (1929-1985). Cowgill's dazzling mastery of the entire Indo-European linguistic world is on full display, with every work a model of expert methodology and depth of thinking." (online)

2   Houghton Mifflin Co., Boston, 1969.

3   There is very little available in English on Heidegger and etymology. I can recommend Matthew King's excellent article "Heidegger's Etymological Method: Discovering Being by Recovering the Richness of the Word," *Philosophy Today,* Fall 2007, pp. 278-289. Thinking etymologically, it seems, "would be in keeping with a poetic kind of writing, a kind of writing that is suggestive rather than demonstrative, a kind of writing that does not make arguments in the manner of philosophy." Inasmuch as Heidegger "wants to move the project of Western thinking beyond 'philosophy,'" a detailed attempt to understand or explain Heidegger's use of etymology is far beyond the scope of this article.

4   *Irrational Man: A Study in Existential Philosophy,* Double Day, New York, 1962, p. 214-215.

5   Paulist Press, New York, 2000.

6   p. 1397

7   Oxford University Press, 1949, p. 738.

8   Judaism 101

9   On this subject see David Hopper, *Technology, Theology, and the Idea of Progress,* Westminster/John Knox Press, 1991, *passim.*

10   Jerome, *His Life, Writings and Controversies,* J.N.D. Kelly, Harper & Row, New York, 1975.

11   This change of short e to short i is commonly called "vowel weakening." The change of a to i in *vaticinor* is also an example of "vowel weakening." See "Vowel Changes" in *Latin Grammar* by Charles E. Bennett, Allyn & Bacon, Boston, 1894, #7, p. 6.

12   Online source

CHAPTER IV
The World's Weirdest Words

There is no shortage of interest in weird words. *The American Heritage Dictionary of the English Language* defines "weird" as "strikingly odd or unusual, especially in an unsettling way; strange." The word "weird" comes from Middle English *werd, wird,* meaning "fate." Ultimately it is from Proto-Indo-European "wer," "turn, bend." At the end of this chapter there is a bibliography consisting of six works all of which deal with "weird words." My approach is to present a few examples from each book.

Mrs. Byrne's Dictionary of Unusual, Obscure, and Preposterous Words (The Citadel Press, 1974) which has recently been republished as *The Indispensabler Dictionary of Unusual Words* (Skyhorse Publishing (1944, 2012):

> Crithomancy - "divining the future by scattering grain, meal, or flour on sacrificial animals." From Greek *krithe,* barley and *manteia,* divining the future, prophesying. (There are hundreds of words ending in -mancy.)

> Creophagous - Corresponds exactly to "carnivorous" which is from Latin *caro, carnis,* "flesh" and *vor-* "eat." *Creo-* is from the Greek word for "flesh," and *phag-* means "eat."

> Crapulence - Latin *crapulentus > crapula,* "drunk" > Greek *kraipale* "a drinking bout," "intoxication"

> Cheimaphilic - "fond of winter." *Cheima* is the Greek word for "frost" and "winter." *Phil-* means "love" in Greek and the suffix *-ic* means pertaining to.

Disboscation - deforesting, clearing forest land

Eleutheromania - a mania for freedom

Flummadiddle - a New England holiday dish consisting of stale bread, pork fat, molasses, cinnamon and cloves

Hepaticocholangiocholecystenterostomy - surgically created link between the gall bladder and the hepatic duct and between the intestine and gall bladder.

The Superior Person's Book of Words by Peter Bowler:

Aeaeae, "magic." The name of the island off the coast of Italy where Circe lived. When Odyseus landed there, she turned his men into pigs. The etymology of aeaeae is unknown.

Ante-jentacular, "before breakfast." Personally I never do much before breakfast except get out of bed. Hence I won't be using this word. I much prefer a postprandial circumambulation.

Cacophemism is the opposite of euphemism which is a kind way of stating something. e. g. "He passed away" instead of "He died." A cacophemism is a crude or blunt expression. *Eu-* is a Greek prefix that means "good" or "well." *Caco-* is the opposite. Cf. euphony and cacophony.

Chrematophobia. This is just one of hundreds of phobias and most likely one of the rarest. It is the fear of money. I personally have never met a crematophobe. All of my acquaintances are "chrematophiles," to coin a word.

Comiconomenclaturist. "A specialist in funny names."

Gongoozler. "One who stares for hours at anything..."

Nullibiety. "The state of being nowhere." From Latin *nullus,* "no, none," *ibi,* "there," and *-ety* which forms abstract nouns.

Thelyphthoric. "That which corrupts women." From *thely-* one of the Greek words for woman and *pthora,* corruption, decay. While this word is not in the largest Greek dictionary, it is a perfectly good coinage.

Totally Weird and Wonderful Words edited by Erin McKean:

Anopisthograph, "written on only one side."

Atrabilious, "melancholy or bad-tempered." Notice that "atrabilious" is the Latin equivalent of "melancholy." Both mean "black bile."

Catoptromancy, "divination (predicting the future) by means of a mirror."

Criticaster, "an incompetent critic." -aster is a "pejorative" suffix.

Dactylonomy, "the science of counting on your fingers." *Dactylos,* Greek for "finger" and -nomy "science of."

Ergophobic, refers to one who is afraid of work." Greek *ergon* (work) is cognate with English "work."

Flarf, coined by a poet to describe really bad poetry.

Ichnomancy, "divination by means of footprints."

Kakistocracy, "rule by the worst citizens." The opposite of aristocracy. *Kakisto-* is the superlative of *kakos,* "bad."

Onolatry, "the worship of donkeys."

2000 Most Challenging and Obscure Words by Norman. W. Schur (563 pp. = Two Vols. in one; a real bargain!) A few examples from the A's and Bs:

Abiosis, "the absence of life"

Absquatulate, "to escape, to decamp, to take off in a hurry"

Aeonian, "everlasting, eternal"

Agitprop, "political propaganda" (especially favoring communism)

Ailurophile, "a cat lover"

Anoesis, "an emotion without cognitive content"

Ataraxia, "freedom from anxiety"

Bahuvrihi, "with much rice" (Sanskrit)

Bathysiderodromphobia, "the dread of subways" (which the parts mean)

Bloviate (slang) "to orate longwindedly"

Foofaraus, "much ado about nothing" or "flashy clothes"

Dickson's Word Treasury: A Connoisseur's Collection of Old and New, Weird and Wonderful Words, Dickson, Paul, (John Wiley & Sons, Inc. 1982)

This marvelous book has thousands of absolutely fascinating words organized into fifty chapters with titles such as Bluff Words, Drinking Words, Journalese, Loutish Words, and Neologisms. It seems appropriate to give a few examples of the author's own coinages from Chapter 12, which is entitled "Dicksonary."

Centicipation, "something that has fallen far below that which had been anticipated; a 99 percent failure."

Fidocanesis, "process by which owners come to look more and more like their pets."

Gnusman, "the ruthless, compulsive punster."

Hojonate, "a one-word compression of a multiworded name for a company, product, or service. From Hojo which is the hojonate of Howard Johnson."

Nork, a product that looks especially appealing in its original context...but that loses all appeal very shortly after you get it.

Nusnobs, unlike your old snobs...nusnobs are "relativists who look down on whatever they are not."

Punburn, "the pain that comes with a pun that has not been expressed."

Where a Dobdob Meets a Dikdik: A Word Lover's Guide to the Weirdest, Wackiest, and Wonkiest Lexical Gems by Bill Casselman

This is a fascinating book, as one might surmise from the subtitle. Words are organized into chapters with title such as "Names and Nincompoops," "Names Get Even Odder," "Edible Words," "Creepy Words," and "Putting the *Sippi* in Mississippi and the *Michi* in Michigan."

A dobdob is a "punk monk" in a Tibetan lamasery."

A dikdik is "a tiny, dainty-hoofed African antelope."

A ning-nong is "a fool or stupid person." The word is still alive in New Zealand and Australian slang. Other gems: "Husqvarna: The Most Mispronounced Company Name in the World."

Depraved and Insullting English by Peter Novobatzky and Ammon Shea (St. Martin's Press, New York, 1999)

One cannot describe this book better than the authors themselves have done: "The words contained in this book were judged worthy of inclusion on many grounds. Some were lascivious, some were mildly derogatory, and others were utterly revolting. A few were all of these things." I need not say anything further.

Anorchus - "Having no testicles."

Blenorrhea - "The morbid and excessive secretion of mucus."

Cacocallia - "The state of being ugly but sexy."

Cicisbeo - "The young male/lover/escort/admirer of a married lady."

Dysania - "Difficulty getting out of bed in the morning."

Ergophobia - "Hatred or fear of work."

Suoid - "hoglike"

,Vocabula Bound: Outbursts, Insights, Explanations, and Oddities: Essays on the English Language from The Vocabula Review, Robert Hartwell Fiske

Rhinothetic - "Having a tendency to stick one's nose in other people's business."

Bisedilious - "Pertaining to a bus rider or theatergoer so large that two seats are necessary to accommodate him or her."

Podostomatic - "Tending to suffer from foot-in-mouth disease."

Kerysomnia - "The unfailing ability to fall asleep during a sermon."

[These are rich and rewarding books which contain many "unsolicited remarks from readers of *The Vocabulary Review.*"

Amazing Words, An Alphabetical Anthology of Alluring, Astonishing, Astounding, Bedazzling, Beguiling, Bewitching, Enchanting, Enthralling, Entrancing, Magical, Mesmerizing, Miraculous, Tantalizing, Tempting, and Transfixing Words, Richard Lederer

Charactonym - "The name of a literary character that is especially suited to his or her personality," e.g., Scrooge, Mr. Gradgrind, Dr. Dryasdust

Chocoholic (also with "-holic" meaning "one addicted to" e.g., work-, news-, word-, shop-, and "spenda-"

"Group nouns" e.g. a barren of mules, a charm of finches, a clowder of cats, a convocation of eagles, a crash of rhinoceroses, an exaltation of larks, a gaggle of geese, a murmuration of starlings, a parliament of owls, and many more.

Floccinaucinihilipilification - "the categorization of something as worthless or trivial."

Word Workout: Building a Muscular Vocabulary in 10 Easy Steps by Charles Harrington Elster

As an online advertisement says, "Far more than a cram session for a standardized test, this book is designed as a lifetime vocabulary builder, featuring words used by the top tier of literate Americans, laid out in ten accessible chapters designed for anyone who is looking for some serious verbal exercise." Examples of words discussed in the 492 pages of this book: anachronistic, detritus, dossier, hubris, emblematic, nefarious, ambrosia

Also by Mr. Elster, *There's a Word for It: A Grandiloquent Guide to Life* with chapters entitled: "Frightful Words," "Snollygosters and Quomodocunquizers," and "Doodads, Rigamjigs, and Whatnots." A few examples of weird words: cachinnation, gweek-gwak, polyphloisboian, tirl, and wheeple.

Who Put the Butter in Butterfly? David Feldman and Kassie Schwan

Strictly speaking this is not a book about weird words, but it is a very charming book in the course of which the author discusses many words; hence I am including it here. Here are some questions the author raises and answers:

Why Are Laudatory Quotations on a Book Cover Called *Blurbs*?

Why is Something Great, a "Real Knockout," Called a *Doozy*?

Why is a Leader or Boss Called a *Honcho*?

Why are Jitters called the *Heebie Jeebies*?

Does Anyone Ever Engage in *Low Jinks*? And What's a *Jink*?

Why Are Fraudulent Healers Known as *Quacks*?

The Completely Superior Person's Book of Words, Peter Bowler. This volume (consisting of 383 pages) combines three of Bowler's earlier books: *The Superior Person's Book of Words, The Superior Person's Second Book of Words, The Superior Person's Third Book of Words*. Not included is his *The Superior Person's Field Guide to Deceitful, Deceptive & Downright Dangerous Language.*

Aasvogel - A vulture

Absquatulate - To leave in a hurry, suddenly, and/or in secret.

Aeaeae - Magic. As in *aeaeae artes,* the magic arts.

Alopecia - Spot baldness

Blennophobia - A morbid dread of slime

Comiconomenclaturist - A specialist in funny names

In a Word. A Dictionary of Words That Don't Exist but Ought To. Jack Hitt, editor

I have great respect for the author of this book. This is because I once set out to coin some words and couldn't think of even one. This is a book of 185 pages which, estimating conservatively at five words per page, has nearly 1,000 words "that don't exist but should." Here are a few, chosen randomly.

Acquend n. [acquaintance + friend] "Someone who is more than an acquaintance but less than a friend."

Affluential adj. [affluent & influential] "Having influence through great wealth..."

"Antisummitism" n. [anti- + summit + -ism}: An attitude of fixed antagonism, suspicion or hostility towards gatherings of national or international political figures..."

"Apodiabolism n [apotheosis + *diabolus,* devil]: An act of making a devil of someone..."

"Arsurdity n. [*ars,* art, + *surd,* deaf, mute...incapable of expression] The unexplainable or irrational in art..."

"Bodywit n [*body & wit*] The subconscious mind of the body..."

The Etymologicon: A Circular Stroll Through the Hidden Connections of the English Language by Mark Forsyth

"The popularity of *Inky Fool* led to Forsyth's first book publishing deal in 2011 with Icon Books. In *The Etymologicon: A Circular Stroll Through the Hidden Connection of The English Language*, Forsyth explains the meanings and derivations of well-known words and phrases, and explores the strange connections between words in a stream-of-consciousness fashion. The book's title, originally called *Point Blank Check Mate: The Inky Fool's Book of Word Association*, refers to the poet John Milton, who purportedly invented the word "etymologicon" to describe a book containing etymologies. The book's structure, described as whimsical, leads the reader to unexpected coinages and devious linkages, sexy, learned and satisfyingly obscure." Wikipedia

The Joy of Lex, An Amazing and Amusing Z to A of Words and A to Z of Words by Gyles Brandreth, (Chapters go from Z to A and then A to Z.)

Xenodocheionology - "The lore of hotels and inns."

Embourgeoisification (no definition given)

Hyperlipoproteinemia (no definition given)

Pachycephalosaurian (no definition given)

Franglification - "The introduction of English words and expressions into French."

Jagonaut - "A person who uses jargon excessively"

Blaxploitation (no definition given)

Counterklutzical (no definition given)

Humuhumunukunukuapuaa - "A small Hawaiian fish"

The Dictionary of Disagreeable English, A Curmudgeon's Compendium of Excrutiatingly Correct Grammar by Robert Hardwell Fiske, (Writer's Digest Books, 2005)

Alphabeticalize - Solecistic for alphabetize.

Amongst - Solecistic for among.

Braggadocious - "Idiotic for boastful."

Differential - Misused for difference.

Embetterment - Idiotic for betterment.

Enthuse - Solecistic for excite.

Exceptionable - misused for exceptional.

Anguished English: An Anthology of Accidental Assaults upon Our Language by Richard Lederer (Dell Publishing)

Police Begin Campaign to Run Down Jaywalkers

Flaming Toilet Seat Causes Evacuation at High School

Two Convicts Evade Noose; Jury Hung

Drunk Gets Nine Months in Violin Case

New Housing for Elderly Not Yet Dead

Prostitutes Appeal to Pope

British Left Waffles on Falkland Islands

Lawyers Give Poor Legal Advice

Additional Bibliography

Peter Bowler and Leslie Cabarga *The Superior Person's Field Guide to Deceitful, Deceptive and Downright Dangerous Language*

Peter Bowler, *The Superior Person's Second Book of Weird and Wondrous Words*

Gyles Brandreth, *More Joy of Lex: A celebration in Praise and Pun of the English Language*

Robert Hartwell Fiske, *Silence, Language & Society*

Phyllis R. Martin, *Word Watcher's Handbook: A Deletionary of the Most Abused and Misused Words*

Mitchell Symons, *The Weird World of Words*

WÖRDOS

The English language super sleuths.

May 16, 2006

(Wördos? A loosely organized group of friends who like to meet and talk about words. ST = Mpls Star Tribune, PP = St. Paul Pioneer-Press, NYT = New York Times, unatt = don't know source, undtd = don't know date, re = regarding, head = headline, ed = editor, AHD = American Heritage Dictionary III, YFIO = you figure it out. DCLN: Didn't catch last name. Italics used freely for emphasis. All entries contributed by Wördos, all dates 2006's unless flagged. Contributions are welcome!)

Spring grabbers:

"Jesus standing before Pontius *Pilot*." (Burnett Co. [Wis.] Sentinel, 3-3-'04)
"Shalom Baptist *To Present Jews For Jesus' Last Supper*" (Head, Glencoe Enterprise, 3-21)
"The cause of the avalanches is being blamed on *heavy snow*." (BBC, 3-28)
"She was able to *overcome her struggle* with bulimia." (Fox News, 2-24)
"*Wall-to-wall* citizens crowded into the auditorium." (WCCO-News, 3-22)

"The Bemidji choir has gained international *notoriety*."
(Exc. & Shorewood Sun-Sailor, 3-30)
"She said the responses haven't been divided between Lake Virginia
residents wanting to increase *the opening to Smithtown Bay residents*
wanting to keep it the same." (Lakeshore Wkly News, 4-11.YFIO)
"The Elks Lodge will hold a *cancer and youth auction*
at 1 p.m. today." (Owatonna PP, undtd, '06)
"Immigrants who *literally planted themselves*
there." (A&E Cable Network, 11-5-'05)
"The car *allegedly* struck a utility pole." (Owatonna P-P, 4-20.
Caption for a photo showing a car wrapped around a utility pole.)
"Minneapolis is creating a *homeless coalition*."
(Amelia Santaniello, CH4, 4-3)

Strategies and *initiatives:* what do they mean?

I asked eleven persons, all with four-year college degrees, what those two
words meant in the sentence: *"Strategies and initiatives are going forward."* Four of
the 11 made a distinction between *strategy* and *tactics:* i.e., between a long-range
goal and the means to achieve the goal. The four were an office manager, a 3M
sales executive, an advertising executive, and a librarian. All said they used the
strategy-tactics distinction in their work. The other seven believed that *strategy*
and *plan* had roughly the same meaning. Two comments: *"Plan* doesn't sound as
good," and "A *strategy* isn't any plan, it's *our* plan – one we've worked out to reach
an objective." None of the eleven could give a concise definition of *initiative.*
Several described it vaguely as signifying movement or action.

The distinction between *strategy* (the "what," to win the war) and *tactics* (the
"how," win with air power) is clear and useful in the military profession. When
words spread from technical to public usage their original (and this case, their
effective) meanings often are lost. It's the application of Bernstein's Second Law
again: "Bad words tend to drive out good ones, and then they do, the good ones
never appreciate in value, sometimes maintain their value, *but most often lose in
value, whereas the bad words may remain bad or get better."* (The Careful Writer,
Theodore Bermstein, 1975)

Oxford English Dictionary, 1971: *"Strategy:* The art of a commander-in-chief;
the art of projecting and directing the larger military movements of a campaign,
usually distinguished from *tactics,* which is the art of handling forces in battle. A
plan of action or policy. *Initiative:* First step in some process or enterprise." RMS.

Alright is not all right: "Saturday Night's *Alright!*" (AARP Bulletin, March)

Belies: meaning, please? "Andersen's Compassion *Belies* Building Dedication" (Head, Anoka Co. Union, 3-24. AHD: "*Belies:* To picture falsely, to misrepresent." Exactly bass-ackward.)

Consumers and customers: Not the same. *Customers* apply to persons who buy from, or patronize an establishment on a regular basis. But *consumers* (AHD) relates to persons who consume, in particular those who acquire goods or services for direct use, not for sale.

Few-less: "A *few less* gray hairs." (Northwestern Ins. Co. ad, undtd) "*Less* (FEWER!) than 201 Dist. 883 residents voted." (S. Crow River News, 11-14-'05) "The military hopes to have *less* (FEWER!) than 100,000 troops in Iraq ..." (ST, 11-23-'05)

Hate words & phrases: "He will ***graduate college.***" "They ***declined comment.***" (Ned Crabb, Wall St. Jnl, 11-24-'05) ***It's about,*** as in "We're about helping you get what you want." (New Yorker, 3-20) "Everything about this camera *is about* picture quality. (Am. Store ad, Cable TV, 3-29) "We're not about shoes, we're about rock." (King of the Hill, unatt, 4-2) ***Ability*** instead of ***can:*** "A woodcock *has the ability to* (can) open just its (bill) end." (Outdoor News, 4-7) "The defense attorney *has the ability to know* (knows) how the thing works." (ST quote, 3-22) "*Having the ability to* (It can) locate fish." (Outdoor News, 4-7) "She *gave them the ability* (She helped them) to go to the inside." (ESPN announcer, 4-2) Thanks for these to Wordo Fred Webber.)

Huh? "Was *Siting* (Sighting!) Really An Ivory-billed Woodpecker?" (Head, ST, 3-17) "Perhaps if Kapil were not so *broadly abled* ..." (ST, 2-20. YFIO) "We *squash* an e-mail rumor ..." (Connie Nelson, ST, 3-8, was asked about this. She responded: "You're right. I was attempting to play on words.") "Zygi Wolf called Hubbard Broadcasting ... to *squash* the story." (ST, 1-5-'05. This one, apparently, was committed intentionally.) "Must be 21." (Ad, Owatonna PP, 3-2. For 21-year-olds only.) Carley Simon introduces us to an *extended member of her family."* (CH5, undtd. He's the big and fat one.) "(They all) donated time and energy to complete the *install."* (Deephaven school report, winter, '05) "About 600,000 acres, teens have plenty of room to hunt and fish and ride ATVs and snowmobiles." (ST, 3-20) "His (Goebbels) *reverberations* that the Jewish people are a menace ..." (ST, 2-12. *Reverberate:* to resound, as if in a succession of echoes. To reecho.") "With their eyes *agog."* (David [last name?], CH2, 3-3) "We *beseeched* several groups for funding." (C-Span, 2-26) "Man Convicted Twice ..." (ST, 4-11. Story says he was convicted three times.) "Nobel Peace *Price"* (Lakeshore Wkly News, 2-28)

Poetry corner: *A Sam's Club clerk got my advice, /A simple word change would suffice./ No, nothing hard or grim or dour, / Just change the word from "less" to "fewer." He did not have to yell or bawl./ He gave a look that said it all./ A look from which I quickly learned / That he was terribly concerned. (Wordo Ray Warner)*

Pushed back: a flat contradiction! "Three meetings have been *pushed back* (NO! They have been *postponed!*) in order to allow more time..." (PP, 11-30) "Mesaba Airlines ... agreed Tuesday to *push back* the judge's deadline." (Liz Fedor, ST, 3-15. Wordo Ray Warner wrote Ms. Fedor: "For heaven's sake, banish *push back* forever and substitute *postpone.* Are you under the impression that time marches *backward?"*)

Position of words in the sentence: "Baseball doesn't *just* belong to America" (Head, ST, 3-18. "Baseball doesn't belong *just* to America"?)

Spelling errors: simple typo or simple ignorance? "Woman Uses *Fony* $100 To Pay For Girl Scout Cookies:" (Owatonna PP, 3-8) "Nobel Peace *Price"* (Lakeshore Wkly News, 2-28) "Not that that seems to *phase* (faze) Ms. Jones...) (NYT, 2-15) "I love to sit in the stately, no-nonsense reading room *boarded* (bordered?) on two sides by stacks." (Rudy Maxa, ST, 2-19) "Older Americans Not Working So Late In Life

As *Formally*. (Hibbing Dly Tribune, 3-10) "Claude Jones takes *awhile* (a while)." (City Pages, 2-22) "(The office) has been abused *to* long." (Rep. Party e-mail, 3-30) "The gas *peddle* is on the floor." (ST, 3-16) "MacMahon *honed* (homed) in on FBI mistakes." (ST, 3-21)

Temperatures do not get warmer or colder. They go up or they go down: "The global trend of *warmer* (ocean temperatures) …it all started with *warmer* sea temperatures…" (Smith Borenstein, AP, 3-31)

Words, useful but seldom seen: "(Her new novel) focuses on the *fraught* mother …" (NYT, 4-9. "*Fraught:* marked by distress." (AHD)

— yr humble & obt svt, Robert MacGregor Shaw

WÖRDOS

The English language super sleuths.

June 12, 2006

(Wördos? A loosely organized group of friends who like to meet and talk about words. ST = Mpls Star Tribune, PP = St. Paul Pioneer-Press, NYT = New York Times, WSJ = Wall St. Jnl., unatt = don't know source, undtd = don't know date, re = regarding, head = headline, ed = editor, AHD = American Heritage Dictionary III, YFIO = you figure it out, DCLN: Didn't catch last name. Italics used freely for emphasis. All entries contributed by Wördos, all dates 2006 unless flagged. Contributions are welcome!)

Detours and Roadblocks

"A Midwestern outdoorsman, Charlie fell in love
with mountains in college and hasn't stopped
climbing since," (ST obit, 4-26). Yes, he has.
"The *self-confessed* murderer..." (CH4, 4-25).

"He's the right man to lead the CIA at this critical moment in
our nation's history... he will provide outstanding leadership to
meet the challenges and threats of a dangerous new century,"
(Pres. Bush nominating Gen. Michael Hayden
as CIA director, 5-8-2006).

"He's the right man to lead this important agency at this critical moment in our nation's history... (he is on) an essential mission to lead the agency for the challenges and threats of a dangerous new century,"
(Pres. Bush, nominating Porter Goss as CIA director, 8-'10-'04).

★   ★   ★   ★

Agreement, lack of: "...handful of volunteers *have* (has) signed up," (ST, 4-19). "Find the person who predicted (it) and *they'll* (he will) show you," (Joe Christiansen, ST, 4-20). "*Here's* (here are) the seven bottom teams," (ST, 4-20). "The algae that *causes* black streaks or stains..." and "The algae *tends* (tend) to flourish..." (Karen Youso, ST, 4-25). AHD: *Alga*= singular, *algae*= plural. "Bacteria that *travels* (travel)," (KTNF AM Radio commercial, 5-15) *Bacterium* = singular, *bacteria* = plural. "Members recommended that anyone interested in donating *their* (his) body to science..." (ST, 5-3). "...turmoil among *he* (him) and his partners," (Graydon Boyce, ST, 5-13). "Only 1 in 4 people *are* (is) confident *they* (he, she, he or she, or recast) have enough for retirement," (The Hartford Co. ad, unatt.).

Ambiguous reference: "After sticking (inoculating) the mother bear and waiting for the drug to take effect, the female's yearly cub poked her head out of the den and retreated," (ST, 3-12). This says the cub inoculated his mother. "...tracked down the car near a Kansas city home *with the Minnesota license place still attached,*" (WCCO-TV, 5-2). It wasn't the house with the attached license plate, it was the car. "As I gripped the wheel of the car tighter, *it hit me* in a way that still brings tears to my eyes," (Minn. Senior News, 4-'06). Don't grip it so tightly next time.

Few-less: "A *few less* gray hairs," (Northwestern Ins. Co. ad, undtd). "*Less* (**fewer!**) than 201 Dist. 883 residents voted," (S. Crow River News, 11-14-'05). "The military hopes to have *less* (FEWER!) than 100,000 troops in Iraq..." (ST, 11-23-'05).

Hate words & phrases: (From discussion at Wördos meetings): "He will *graduate college,*" and "They *declined comment,*" (Ned Crabb, Wall St. Jnl, 11-24-'05). *Mom:* "(The pianist) Jie Chen lives with her *mom,*" (Minn. Piano-e-comp newsltr, 4-'06). *Preventatively:* "A lot can be done *preventatively,*" (Commonwealth, 2-'06). *Conjoin,* as in "words that are *conjoined* together." (Why not simply *join?*)

Huh? "What's the difference between a 7-pound, 3-ounce baby and a 3,300 kilogram baby? They are the same," (Rochester P-B, quoting Mayo newsletter, 5-1). Wördo Jeremiah Witt: "No. A 3,300 kilogram baby weighs 7,260 pounds. A 3.3 kilogram baby weighs 7.26 pounds." "Must be 21," (Ad, Owatonna PP, 3-2). For 21-year-olds only. "The Owatonna Elks Club, Lodge 1395 will hold a *dcancer and youth auction* at 1 p.m. today," (Owatonna PP, March, '06). "...he *took* a chemistry degree," (ST, 4-17). Received? "After WWII, marketers *strived* (strove) to create products..." (ST, 4-26). "(It was) extremely well *lawyered,*" (Unatt, 3-26). We find no evidence for the verb "to lawyer." But the *lawyering* is acceptable (AHD) as a noun: "They do most of the *lawyering* in the country." "It was cut and *dry,*" (Commonwealth, 2-'06). "(Our mission was) to collect unexploded *ordinates,*" (Commonwealth, 2-'06). Ordnance. "Mannequins wear... hats with *boutonnieres,*" (Rake, 5-'06). No. They're worn in a button-hole. "...*not* (no) time like the present," (Minn. Senior News, 4-'06). "New U.S., Iran Strategies Could *Escalate Standoff*" (ST, 4-30). Mixed metaphor. Can't quite see a standoff escalating. "And sources familiar with the case have said a plea agreement is being explored," (ST, 5-4). The whole sentence.

Neologisms: New words. Here are the winners of the Washington Post's annual Neolgism Contest. Readers were asked to give alternate meanings to common words. *Coffee:* The person upon whom one coughs. *(2) Flabbergasted:* appalled over how much weight you have gained. (3) Balderdash: a rapidly receding hairline. Readers were also asked to create new words by changing one letter. Winners: (1) Giraffiti: Vandalism spray-painted very, very high. (2) *Sarchasm:* The gulf between the author of sarcastic wit and the person who doesn't get it. (3) *Inoculatte:* To take coffee intravenously when you are running late.

Only: "It *only happens* (No! It happens only) once a year," (New Yorker, undtd, ad for Starbucks Coffee). "Childress's desire to become the Vikings coach might *only have been surrpassed by owner Zygi Wilf's desire...*" (ST, 1-7). No. "...might have been surpassed *only* by owner..."

-osis: An editorial in WSJ, 4-26, had the playful headline *Litigosis*. Describing tort abuse in the courts, WSJ wrote: "Only when judges police their own courtrooms... will the U.S. rid itself of its worst disease: *litigosis*." Response from Prof. Jeremiah Reedy: "The suffix *-osis* in Greek forms an abstract noun and denotes condition or process as in *osmosis, metamorphosis, sclerosis.*" AHD lists as the second meaning of *-osis:* "diseased or abnormal condition."

Scot-free, Scotch, Scottish: *Scot-free* has nothing to do with Scotland. It comes from a Scandinavian word meaning "free of royal tax." Scotch is a kind of whiskey. People who live in Scotland are Scots. They are *Scottish.*

Spelling: "Woman Uses *Fony* $100 To Pay For Girl Scout Cookies" (Owatonna PP, 3-8). The all-time winner: "Jesus standing before Pontius *Pilot,*" (Burnett Co. [Wis.] Sentinel, 3-3-'04). "...taking the *omelet* off the griddle," (PP, 3-16). "Nobel Peace *Price*" (Lakeshore Wkly News, 2-28). "Sabo Leaves Successor A *Sizable* Legacy To Fill," (ST, 3-27).

Subjunctive: "As if he *was* (were) trying to get a jump on the deer..." (Burnett Co. [Wis.] Sentinel, 11-9-'05). "If Lincoln *was* (were) president today..." (Commonwealth, 2-'06).

TV talk: "...*repartriate them back here...*" (Bill O'Reilley, re deserters in Canada). "A trend toward *realtiy,*" (BBC commentator, 1-4). "She managed to *re-home* the dogs," (Unatt. TV, undtd). "The paths are open to bicycles. They are not open to vehicles." (From Stringer Natty Bumpo, WKYU-FM [W. Kentucky U.], undtd). "...snow melted on contact with the relatively *mild ground*," (Paul Douglas, CH4, 11-16). "Doctors said it couldn't have *went* more smoothly," (Jeanette Trompeter, CH4, 5-12). Carley Simon introduces us to an *extended member of her family*," (CH5, undtd). "There could be *delayment*," (Unatt., 4-20, re New Orleans's levies). "Upwards of close to three inches in some areas," (CH11 Weatherman, undtd.).

WÖRDOS

The English language super sleuths.

November 20, 2007

(Wördos? About 20 persons, most of them retired teachers or journalists, who get together and talk about words - chiefly words that take a beating in the media. Abbreviations: ST = Minneapolis Star Tribune, PP = St. Paul Pioneer Press, NYT = N.Y.Times; WSJ = Wall St. Journal, unatt = don't know source, undtd = don't know date, nwsltr = newsletter, (1-2-3) = 1st- 2d-3d dict. meaning, AHD = Am. Heritage Dict. III, GMAU = Garner's Modern Am. Usage, OED = Oxford Dict. Of Eng. Lang. II, mag = magazine, YFIO = you figure it out. Contributions welcome! We have a Web page: *http://www.Wördos.net.*

Ice on the road

"The boys ... chose a site that was perched on a deck overlooking an idyllic stream. They built a fire *with their grandfather* and roasted hot dogs." (New Brighton Bulletin, 9-5. He didn't burn well. Just skin and bones.)

"Tomb of the *Unknown Replica* Visits Houston" (Tri-County Record, Rushford, Minn., 7-19. Headline, re visit from the "Traveling Tomb of the Unknown Soldier" to Houston's Hoedown Days, July 27-9)

"Thanks For Your *Patients*" (PP, undtd. Words on a highway department sign along Highway 77, following repair work on the Cedar Avenue Bridge. Good slogan for a hospital!)

★　★　★　★

Agreement, and the sad lack of: "When a majority ... *adopt* (adopts) a manifestly ideological agenda." (NYT, 7-26) "... people often report the sensation of floating over their *body* (bodies)." NYT, undtd) "Both *me* (I) and Emily ..." (ltr, ST, 9-23) "...went to a farm with *he* (him)." (Vineeta Sawkar, CH5, ST, 9-23) "...objected to having fabric on their *head* (heads)." (NYer mag, 9-17) "The years have pushed Alan and I (me) apart..." (Mensa nsltr, 8-'07)

Bravos! Good words! "A *cavalcade* of imports from China." (C-span hearing, 10-11) "*Cavalcade:* (1) procession of riders, (2) ceremonial procession, (3) succession or series." (AHD) "The way of life was perfectly *viable*." (CH2 re New Guinea, 10-9. "*Viable:* (1) Capable of living, developing or germinating under favorable conditions. (3) Capable of success." (AHD) "There are *externalities* in this." (Pres. of Del. St. U., re campus shooting, 9-21. AHD 4th ed blesses this usage.)

Cliches and latest fads: *Ability,* as in "Now you have the *ability* (opportunity? chance?) to do what you want." (Bank of Am. nsltr, 9-28) Other miscreants: ***"It goes without saying," "opening Pandora's box,"*** and ***"sliding down the slippery slope."*** "Modern writing at its worst does not consist in picking out words for the sake of their meaning and inventing images in order to make the meaning clearer. It consists in gumming together long strips of words (that) have already been set in order by someone else, and making the results presentable by sheer humbug." (George Orwell, *Politics and the English Language*.)

Fraught, without *with*: "... resurgent spirits after the *fraught* Winter Line campaign." (Rick Atkinson, "The Day of Battle.") "*Fraught*: marked by distress, upsetting." (AHD) *Fraught* without the preposition *with* gives us a subtle change in meaning. The traditional *fraught with* suggests "loaded with" in accordance with the original ME word "to load." Atkinson's *fraught* without *with* I take to mean "unlucky, dangerous, deadly." Other *fraughts* without the preposition are also showing up. – Ed.

Huh? "Simultaneous jobs will be done *at the same time.*" (Unatt. TV discussion of bridge plan, 7-12) "Boeing *Pushes Back* (No! Postpones!) Delivery of Dreamliners" (ST, 10-11) "Business has *shrunken* (shrunk)." (PP comic, undtd. AHD, fourth ed. accepts *shrunken.*) "Toronto 6, Boston 1 ... as the *visiting* Blue Jays defeated the *visiting* Red Sox." (ST, 9-20) "He has three touchdown passes *on the day.*" "The only blind man to *summit* Mt. Everest." (NBC News, 9-24. Wordo Fred Webber points out that AHD 4th ed. blesses this usage.) "The *criteria* (criterion) ... seemed to be this." (Judd Zulgad, ST, 9-21) "Tigers ... in the African grasslands." (TV Guide, 9-29. Nope. Not in Africa) "Is going *further* (farther) for heart care ...important?" (Park-Nic. ad, ST, 10-4) "... he *laid* (lay) unconscious." (ST, 10-9) "He was known for a *succinct baritone.*" (PP, undtd) "... relatives speculate (it) was *the reason why* (the reason) ..." (ST, 9-6)

Parameter – perimeter: Commonly confused. *Parameter* has the sense of *restriction,* as its correct use in "A zoning ordinance that limits the height of new buildings includes planning *perameters.* But, as Wordo Ray Warner says, "*Parameter* is often used as a high-toned synonym for *characteristic.* It resembles the word *perimeter* and with it shares the sense of limit, but *perimeter* does not connote restriction."

Politics: Singular or plural? "*Politics are* (is) simply ingrained into the culture." "*Politics,* although etymologically plural, takes a singular verb when referring to the art or science of governing ... but in other senses it can take either a singular or a plural noun." (AHD)

Preposition problems: "(The report) *into* (about) mass killings ... is amazing." (Spectator Mag., 7-23) Bert Blyleven, in commenting on Twins games, says "Ten hits *on* (for?) the year." "(Soldiers) posing

in front of Armenians they hung *on* (in) a public place." (ST, undtd)
(Wördo Ray Warner: "Sports reporters have adopted a puzzling choice
of preposition in *on the day*. Wouldn't *for* the day be better?")

Pronunciation: *"Politicalization* (U.S. Sen. Bob Graham, unatt.,
inserts the unnecessary syllable into *politicization*.) "... removed blockage
in his (pause) *car- roid* (**carotid**) artery." (CNN, 10-13)

Spelling goofs: Hit the wrong key or was it ignorance? *"Protential
delays"* (CH5 graphic, 9-24) "... *Stugary* (Stuttgart), Germany." (PP
ad, 9-30) "Men under 30 *faired* (fared) the worst." (PP, 9-14) "...
occasionally firing off *canons* (cannons)." (Writer's Almanac, 8-21) "...a
palace complete with a *mote* (moat)." (ST caption, 9-2)

TV, radio people: Oh, listen how they talk: "Men and women
waiting for *a haircut* (haircuts.") (NPR, 8-23) "Everyone, young and
old, *enjoy* (enjoys) the spectacle." (BBC, 10-4) "No *official* date has
been set..." (Korva Coleman, NPR, 9-24. Stringer Natty Bumppo:
"Use of *official* here is superfluous and wrong.") "(Expert) talks of new
regime (regimen) for dealing with depression." (NPR, 8-15) "I really felt
badly (bad)..." (Syl Jones, MPR, 10-12) "It's a situation *well familiar* to
those following the story." (NPR, 10-8) "... off Douglas *Road* (Drive)."
(Chris Keating, CH5, 9-21) *"Fairway* (Fairview) Ave." (Ad for ½ Price
Books opening.) "Booking Fee *Waved"* (waived) (CH5 graphic, 9-27.
Thanks to Stringer Bill Farmer.) "Years of delay *have* (has) made it..."
(CH5, 9-24)

Wake-woke (or waked) – waked (or woken): "Research subjects are
periodically *awoken...*" (NYT, 10-23) "Americans have *woken up."* (Al
Franken mailer, undtd. Either *waked* or *woken* is correct, according
to AHD, as the past participle of *wake*. "The pairs *wake – woken*
and *awake-awaken* have formed a bewildering array since the Middle
English period." Ergo, both NYT's and Franken's quotes are correct.)

Words seldom, if ever, seen: ***Soda pop.*** (NYT, 7-24. In the Midwest, it's *pop.*) ***Epicist,*** as in "... that *epicist* of the female experience." (NYT, 10-12. No sign of it in AHD) ***Gyre,*** as in "If Afghanistan is to move from its destructive *gyre.*" (NYT, 10-22. "*Gyre:* A circular or spiral form, a vortex." AHD) ***Overwatching,*** as in "Our troops will shift ... to *overwatching* these forces." (Pres. Bush, 9-13. "A strategy for observing nearby so as to back a fighting ally." (William Safire, NYT, 10-14)

— yr humble & obt svt, Robert MacGregor Shaw

WÖRDOS

The English language super sleuths.

December 12, 2006

Wördos? A loose organization of friends who love to talk about words. Abbreviations: ST = Mpls Star Tribune, PP = St. Paul Pioneer-Press, NYT = New York Times, WSJ = Wall St. Jnl., OED = Oxford Dictionary of English Lang., AHD = American Heritage Dictionary III, WEG = Warriner's Eng. Grammar & Composition, YFIO = you figure it out. UM = unidentified miscreant. Italics used freely for emphasis. Unatt = don't know source, undtd = don't know date, head = headline, all entries contributed by Wördos, all dates 2006's unless flagged. Contributions welcome! We have a Web page: http://Wördos.net/stats/index.html. From 6-13 to 9-18.

Merry Christmas!

Two very good words, and with them the Wördos – about 20 of them, many who worked in the mass media – wish *particularly* to greet all the suffering-but-happy persons who put forth other good words before the public. What a responsibility! From time to time, what fun! "Newspaper work will kill you in the end, but until it does it will keep you *greatly alive.*" (E.W.Scripps)

Corrections: I failed to attribute a quote in Nov. 14's column concerning the vulgar *s-blank-blank-blank* word attributed to Pres. Bush. It was part of an overheard remark he made to England's Prime Minister Tony

Blair at a July, '06 meeting in Moscow. I also failed to identify a new abbreviation: "UM." It stands for "Unidentified Micreant."

★   ★   ★   ★

Ambiguous reference: "Last night upon returning home, a fox was standing at the SW corner of 18th and Comstock." (Chelsea Wood Trails newsletter, 10-'06) "(He was ordered by the court) to stay away fro his family after his wife alleged he *abused drugs and threatened them.*" (ST, 1-28)

Begs the question: *"This begs several questions."* (Joe Soucheray, KSTP Radio, 12-12-05). Wördo Fred Webber: This is not what 'begs the question' means. An argument is a form of reasoning in which one gives a reason or reasons in support of some claim. The reasons are called premises, and the claim one tries to support with them is called the conclusion. If one' premises entail one's conclusion, and one's premises are questionable, one is said to *beg the question.*"

Fads, emerging: *Gravitas,* meaning "weighty seriousness" was around for awhile this spring with reference to Pres. Bush's nominee John Roberts, but seems to have disappeared. *Fraught* is up-and-coming. "... unclear what the pope's reversal will have on the *fraught* debate." "(The pope's visit to Turkey) was bound to be *fraught*, even before (his) comments in September." (Both NYT, 11-29) AHD lists three meanings: (1) "fully provided", (2) charged, as in "an incident *fraught* with danger", and (3) marked by distress, as "a *fraught* mother-daughter relationship."

Huh? *Troops:* strange word. It can be singular ("a Boy Scout *troop*"), plural ("four *troops* were injured today"), but it cannot refer to a single individual ("one *troop* was injured." "(D.B.) and *the late (A.B.)* announce the marriage of their son." "Ellison and his Qur'an Get Wingnuts Whirling." (ST, 12-2. AHD *"Wing nut:* "A (metal) nut with winglike projections for thumb & forefinger leverage." Seems to be a new idiom.) (Lakeshore Wkly News, 11-7) "(We will not post a letter) until we receive a second letter that *rebukes* (refutes) the first." (Highland Villager, undtd) "(The behavior) was *almost similar* to that of animals..." (Ivanhoe Newswire, undtd) "Davis, a *retiring lawyer...*" (PP, 11-1. Real shy guy.) "Youngdahl said ..." (ST, 11-8. Who Youngdahl? Not mentioned elsewhere.) "Coleman denied touching the accuser's *public hair.* (Wow. That's a switch. Generally *public* gets misspelled.) (Owatonna P-P, 8-2) "The University of North Dakota was abducted more than two years ago and slain." (ST, 7-5) "...date was *pushed back* from 2010 to 2014." (Barb Obershaw, Sun-Current, 3-3. No it wasn't. The date was postponed, advanced, pushed ahead.)

Lie-Lay-Laid: "The Mutual Fund manager will *lay* (LIE!) awake worrying about your money, so you don't have to." (Wall St. Week, TV, undtd) "I have to *lay* (LIE!) on the grass!" (Sally Forth comic, 9-3. Wordo Ray Warner: "When I worked at Bell Labs, a colleague asked a technician how she would spend her vacation. 'I'll probably spend my time *laying* on the beach,' she said. 'Be careful,' he replied. '*Laying* on the beach is fattening!'") "He died while *lying* (LAYING) down stopsticks on 194." (Don Shelby, 9-6) "He *laid* (LAY!) on his back." (ST, 5-23)

Metaphors, good ones: "I have laid pounds of sacrificial chicken tenders across the altar of my expanding waistline." (David Brooks, NYT, 10-8) ""(The report was) couched in anodyne." (NYT, 11-29. *'Anodyne,* AHD: Capable of soothing or eliminating pain.") "She grew on him like she was a colony of E. coli, and he was room-temperature Canadian beef." (one of 2006's annual English-teachers' collection of similies and metaphors.) **And bad ones:** "The chemistry *between* (among) the candidates will be a little taut." (Fox News, 9-19)

Pronunciation goofs: *Electoral* wrongly with an extra syllable, as "EE-lec-TOR-EE-al." Sen. Zell Miller of Georgia said it that way, unatt, undtd). *Fiancee* as "Fee-ANTS" without the final "ay" as, correctly, FEE-on-SAY. (John Sasich, Fox News, undtd. *Fiancee:* woman engaged to be married. *Fiance:* "fi-ANTS", a man engaged to be married.)

Attorney generals instead of *attorneys general*. (Heard repeatedly on MPR before he election.)

Words heretofore unnoticed: ***Edgy,*** as "There hasn't been a comedy this *edgy* in a long time." (Time, 11-6) "*Edgy*: having a sharp or biting edge." (AHD) Helicoptering, as "Doherty ... thinks *helicoptering* (by parents)..." (ST, 9-4) Context seemed to mean parents who hover over their student-children. Can't find. ***Reservating***, "... the *reservating* of Indians." (Morton Marty, KNOW-FM/MPR, 11-5. No can find.) ***Insolation,*** as in "The Times Building expects to save 50% on lighting from ... insolation." (Jack Rosenthal, NYT, 7-16. Insolation: the amount of solar radiation reaching a given point on earth, measured by watts per square meter. We'll be hearing a lot about that word. ***Utopianly,*** as "If Congress could come together ... let's say *utopianly*... (NYT, 12-8. Can't find).

Words we had to look up: ***Elegiac:*** (NYT, 11-2) AHD: "Having to do with mourning. From Gr. *Elegos:* mournful song.") ***Snarkey***, as in "...an Easterner's *snarky* take." (WSJournal, undtd. Can't find in AHD.) ***Hortatory*** AHD: "Marked by exhortation or strong urging." (NYT edit, 11-12) ***Apostasy***, (NYT, 11-12) AHD: "Abandonment of one's religious faith.". ***Thrall,*** as in "held in thrall" (unatt, undtd) AHD: "One who is held in bondage." ("...held in *thrall.*"undtd, unatt.) ***Trope,*** as in "that 'city upon a hill' trope." (ST, 11-23. AHD: "The figurative use of a word or expression ... a figure of speech." ***Wonk:*** (NYT, 11-19) AHD: "A student who studies excessively, a grind." ***Factoid,*** as in "Book full of colorful *factoids.*" (ST, 11-11) AHD: "Unverified or inaccurate information presented to the press as factual." In the example, the writer seems to believe *factoid* means "minor but interesting facts.") ***Valorize:*** (NYT, 11-17) AHD: "To assign a value to."

YFIO: You figure it out. "You will increase your fitness and energy and is tailored to meet the needs of the participants." (Plymouth Sr. Services brochure, undtd) "... and the person *shines you on.*" (ST, 11-10) "This is very much *the cherry at the end of the cake...* (ST, 9-21) "He (Pres. Bush) said he was willing to consider altering his policy when he *received* the recommendations of a partisan policy ... *later this year.*" (ST, 10-25)

— yr humble & obt svt, Robert MacGregor Shaw.

WÖRDOS

The English language super sleuths.

November 14, 2006

Wördos? A loose organization of friends who meet and talk about words. *Logomachy:* (AHD) "A dispute carried on in words only." Abbreviations: ST = Mpls Star Tribune, PP = St. Paul Pioneer-Press, NYT = New York Times, WSJ = Wall St. Jnl., OED = Oxford Dictionary of English Lang., AHD = American Heritage Dictionary III, WEG = Warriner's Eng. Grammar & Composition, YFIO = you figure it out. unatt = don't know source, undtd = don't know date, re = regarding, head = headline, UM = unidentified miscreant. All entries contributed by Wördos, all dates 2006's unless flagged, italics used freely for emphasis. Contributions welcome! We have a Web page: http://Wördos.net/stats/index.html. From 6-13 to 9-18, averaging eight hits a day.)

Goodies

"(D.E.), age 69, went to be with the Lord on Oct. 2d, 2006 in Yuma, Arizona." (ST obit, 10-11) "Kathleen went to be with her Lord on Tues, Sept. 5, 2006 at Methodist Hospital." (ST obit, 9-7. Two recent sightings.) "They were kidnapped *against their wills.*" (Fox News, 8-23. As opposed to being kidnapped by plan or wish.) "(Pres. Bush) visited ...

a wonderful camp for children with chronic diseases established by retired NASCAR star Richard Petty..." (Joe Klein, Time, 10-30. At first reading, this seems to say that Richard Petty established chronic diseases.) "*Plenty* To Debate In Governor's Race" (ST head, p. 1, 11-4. Was this intentional? "That *very destroyed house*." (CH5, 2-15 Uttered by a very dull miscreant.) "Increased patrols in Minneapolis have *enticed* criminals to St. Paul." (CH11, 9-9. *Entice:* To attract by arousing hope or desire." [AHD] St. Paul police were offered to do the *enticing*, but graciously declined.)

Able, have the ability – latest fads: *Able, ability* seem to be replacing the word *can:* "If you want *to be able* to get ..." (Home Shopping Net, 9-19. Want to get.) "At least *get able* to square his shoulders." (NFL commentator, Vikings, unatt., 9-24. Be able.) "If a watch band *has this ability* to wrap around your wrist." (Shop NBC, 10-2. Can wrap.) "If the power goes out, you *have the ability* to hear the weather." (Jim Bakker, TCT Net, 9-30. Can hear.) "... says its stem cells *have the ability to* turn into neural cells." (ST, 9-10. Can turn into.)

Agreement, sad lack of: "... makes an excellent way of holding more condiments into a bun without *them* (THEIR) falling out." (ST, 8-30) "A group ... *are* (IS!) trying to stop development." (ST, 7-18) "Duo *bring* (brings) art sensibility." (ST, 8-28. Collective noun.) "A growing number ... *believe* (BELIEVES!)..." (ST, 8-28) "Neither ... *were* (WAS!) worth the price." (K.Cooper, B Schneier, ST, 9-20) "Heat and humidity *is* (ARE!) indescribable." (Karen Boothe, Rake, June) '...join me in thanking *he* (HIM!) and Jim." (Sen. John Kerry, Fox News, 9-1) "...we swore off criticism of either *he* (HIM!) or Mrs. Clinton." (Barb. Bush, TV, undtd) "When a child is on the Internet, it is hard to protect *them*. (HIM, HER, or in this case IT) (TV ad, N.M. election, 10-6)

Based on – roundly denounced: "Ba*sed on* their qualifications ..." and "... *based on* the court decision." (ST edit, 6-24) "*Based on* their desire to reach labor agreements ..." (ST, 7-22) Some bookish wisdom from writers about usage: "It is as well to avoid using *based on* as a kind of sentence-leading preposition (as in) '*Based on* this assumption, the economy is not expected to improve.' The relationship between *based on* and *the economy* is not a direct one." (Fowler's Modern English Usage). "*Based on* ...fakes a relation between two things when the writer cannot be bothered to see that relation clearly. Hence the epidemic use of the phrase in second-rate writing." (Wensberg, Modern American Usage)

Huh? "...he *got passed* a repeal of vagrancy laws." (Rochelle Olson, ST, 9-5) "(He) *took* a chemistry degree." (ST, 4-17. Didn't have to work or study. Just reached up and took it.) "State Fair runs today through Sept. 4." (ST, 9-4. That would have teen today, 9-4, right?) "Looks like a *shoe-in* (shoo-in)." (PP, 9-22) "...a fellow southerner, Peggy Lee!" (Sat. Night Live, 10-7. Nope. She's from N.D.) "A wonderful Praise-A-Thon." (TCT, 9-27) "...*wise alecks.*" (S. Crow River News, 9-18. Smart-alecks.) "Brewer *loaned* (lent) his laptop." (Chip Scoggins, ST, 10-2) "(Adelman is) entirely disillusioned with the administration's handling of the *postwar.*" (Newsweek, 10-9) "... a failing effort to *stanch* violence in Iraq." (NYT, 10-24. Hey! That's correct! "*Stanch:* To stop the flow of blood ... the variant *staunch* is more common than *stanch* as the spelling of the adjective. *Stanch* is more common than *staunch* as the spelling of the verb." AHD)

Like: (This, from Doug Grow, ST, undtd) "The use of *like* has no meaning, but it seems to serve a variety of purposes. For example, it's a space filler ... fills time and space. The word also softens anything that sounds direct, which makes the Midwest fertile ground for the word to flourish. Tossing in a few *likes* into a sentence serves as a quasi-question. 'It's a way of safeguarding what you say,' says Prof. Lieberman. 'Someone will ask you 'Are you going to teach this course, *like*, next year?' To ask if you're going to teach the course next year is too straightforward ... some people cultivate language as if it's a precious garden. Others, *like*, don't care.'"

Problematic: Its meaning has shifted. Wordo Jeremiah Reedy: "It now conveys great concern. It used to be dismissive. You'd say 'That's *problematic*' with a shrug; now it's with a furrowed brow. It used to be a synonym for *academic* – an interesting sidetrack irrelevant to accomplishing the task at hand. This new *problematic* comes along with a more dithering culture. "... translating that into policy is more *problematic*." (NYT, 11-11. Correct usage: Context indicates that translating into policy would be of concern – poses a problem.)

Public-pubic: There's a difference, a GREAT big difference. "Ottowa County, Michigan will pay about $40,000 to correct 170,000 ballots that were missing the letter 'l' in the word 'public.'" (Center for American Progress, 10-10)

Spelling goofs: "Mr. Reid is also interested *incompleting* the second phase of the ... review." (NYT, 11-8) "Writing a *lede* (or lead) can be ... challenging." (MN Newspaper Found. bulletin, 10-10) Wordo Marlene Reuber noted *pale* for *pail* in a *nukiwi.com* message, complained, and received an answer: "Sending proofreader to do penance on a mountaintop." Reuber responded: "That would be no penance. Send him to L.A." *Gray* or *grey*? AHD lists *gray* as first choice. "Google *payed* (paid) ..." (ST, 10-11) "(He) reviewed several *capitol* (capital) projects." (Walnut Grove, Minn., Sentinel-Trib, 8-23) "...arrested with the *aide* (aid) of police." (Chao Xiong, D. Chanen, ST, 9-29) "...*Falwell* (Folwell) Park." (ST, 10-17) "I welcome him *whole-heartily* (heartedly)." (PP, 6-17)

TV talking heads: "... and that includes you and *I*." (Dennis Douda, CBS local news, 9-4) "Neither *were* (was) impressed." (Sue Turner, CH4, 7-22) "The most rain we're going to see at all." (Fox News, 9-6, UM) "... *fewer* federal taxes to pay." (C-span, 7-21) "The chemistry *between* the candidates will be a little *taut*." (Fox News, 9-19, UM Mixed metaphor!) "The percentage of overweight kids *are* (IS!) increasing." (CH4, 8-15) "... a *wayward* (way) station." (C-Span, 9-10) "Fifty heads of state representing more than 150 countries." (BBC, CH 17, 9-14. YFIO) "... twice as many *than* (as) last year." (NBC, 8-19) "They were *completely* *surrounded."* (NBC, 8-25. As opposed to being partly surrounded.) "The price (cost?) ... will be more expensive." (CH2, 3-7, UM) "(The pill) can help you *gain less weight."* (Maryjane Reagan swears she heard a UM say this on TV, unatt.) "...(was to be) *woken* (waked) at six." (ad, CNN, undtd) "...more *mediums* (media)." (KTNF Radio 9-20). "I'd *borrow* (LEND!) it to you." (Sven Sundgaard, CH11, undtd) "The bus must have *drove* (DRIVEN!) over her." (JoAnne Bemoris, CH5, 9-14)

Vulgarisms on the verge of acceptance? *Slut:* Stephanie Rosenbloom (NYT, reprinted in PP, 8-14) claims that *slut* is now "commonplace in popular culture, marketing, and casual conversations." **Shit, damn:** "What they need to do is get Syria to get Hezbollah to stop doing this *shit* and it's over." and "I'm just going to make it up. Not going to talk too *damn* long like the rest of them." (Pres. Bush, unatt.) **Fart:** "... love on your special day, you old *fart."* (Personal ad, PP, 7-6)

Words, hateful, Wördo Ray Warner is bothered by *over-arching point.* "There's no way that a point can overarch anything – unless it's in motion – and then it becomes a line." Wordo Maryjean Reagan swears she heard a newscaster say "in that *particular situational occasion."* Also from MR: "What has happened to *nod?* I keep hearing 'He shook (not nodded) his head, yes."

– yr humble & obt svt, Robert MacGregor Shaw

Word from the Wördos

November 15, 2005

(Wördos? Friends who like to meet and talk about words; talk about personal health or grandchildren strictly *verboten*. ST = Mpls Star Tribune, PP = St. Paul Pioneer-Press, unatt = don't know source, undtd = don't know date, re = regarding, head = headline, ed = editor, AHD = American Heritage Dictionary III, YFIO = you figure it out. Italics used freely for emphasis. All entries were contributed by Wördos. All dates are 2005's unless flagged. Happenings from Oct.'s meeting: Gleeful clobbering of editor for asserting that correct name of St. Paul's *Regions Hospital* was *Regent's Hospital*. Vigorous pros and cons re ST's new makeover. Words looked up in dictionary: *mope, fettle, tasking, new-fangled*. Discussion about pronunciation of REAL-tor, double meaning of *evacuate*, new book by R. Lederer, historical present in heads.)

"10 items or less" on those check-out signs

Crisis! Crisis! "10 items or less" is back on those checkout signs. Wördos are proud that one of their own (the late Peter Pafiolis) several years ago persuaded Target brass to change *less* to *fewer* in all check-out signs at stores in their system. Disturbing news now comes that Target stores, at least some of them, are reverting to printing *less* instead of *fewer* on those little signs. Wördo Prof. Jeremiah Witt, Winona, and

Wördo Prof. Ray Warner, Edina, confirm the rumor. Jeremiah: "Just checked last night at the Winona Target store. Sure enough. It's *less.*" Ray: "Target store on York Avenue's been doing *less* for some time now. They're particularly insensitive about changing." Jeremiah, again: "Wal-Mart's worse. Every time I go there I mention it, trying to embarrass them. Doesn't help. But Hi-V, Byerly's and Lunds all use *fewer.*" (We spotted one appropriate *fewer* last month: "Keep your comments to 75 words or *fewer...*" (ST, undtd.). Bravo! *Few* is used with items one can *count.*

Agreement, lack of: "But none of them *own* (OWNS!) a car," (New Yorker, 9-12). "What's saving it *are* (IS!) those steel pilings," (CNN, 9-24). "...25 years older than *her* (SHE!)," (S.F. Chronicle, 9-18). "One in five women can't afford it because *they don't* (NO! SHE DOESN'T!) have insurance," (Terri Gruca, CH4, 10-9). "...wide array of weapons *have* (HAS!) been destroyed," (ST, 10-3). "Neither drugs nor robbery *were* (WAS!) involved," (CH11, 10-10). "Nine Inch Nails *Put* (PUTS!) Best Foot Forward," (head, ST, 10-12). N-I-N is name of band, and it's singular. "...there *is* (ARE!) some showers in the forecast," (CH5, 10-14). "The central transaction... *have* (HAS!) never been in dispute," (ST, 9-29).

Ambiguous references: "...he caught a glance at something that startled him *in the front seat,"* (ST, 1-20). "Being a driver's ed teacher, *my desire* is to prepare the next generation..." (Rochester P-B, 8-12). His desire is a driver's ed teacher. "While talking on the phone with... Beth Wellesley in her Edina home office, Puente retrieved a voice mail," (ST, 10-10). (Wördo Fred Webber: "Looks like Wellesley's office is in Edina. Not so. Wellesley's office is in Minneapolis.) "NASA needs to learn the lessons of its past... lessons provided at the cost of the lives of 17 astronauts,' they said, referring to the seven killed aboard Columbia and 10 who died in the Challenger and Apollo I accidents years earlier. *They are members of a 26-person task force..."* (AP story, ST, 8-18). This says that the 17 astronauts who died are members of a task force. "Markarim admitted he had been high on a 'met binge' when he hid in the trunk of a man's car and stabbed him in the throat..." (PP, 4-14).

> *The two items above seem to be the two most common abuses of English committed by local persons who write or talk about the news. "Ambiguous reference," an abuse of good writing style, happens when a writer neglects to read what he or she has written. It should be obvious (see first example, above) that the man was not startled in the front seat. The other, lack of agreement, concerns matching forms between parts of speech: subjects-verbs, prepositions-objects, pronouns-antecedents. In English, these parts of speech must agree with each other in gender, number, and case to make sense. No easy way out, here: enlightenment comes only by serious time with a grammar book. This has nothing to do with correctness, everything to do with clear communication.*

Contronyms: Wördo Prof. Ray Warner: "These are words that have contradictory meanings such as *sanction, cleave, oversight,* and *unqualified.* Another is *discursive* which means, according to my Random House dictionary, 'rambling,' or 'proceeding by reasoning or argument; not intuitive.' A reviewer once observed that my manuscript was 'discursive,' and I thanked him. He then explained that he meant 'rambling.' In 1939 Jerome Kern's musical play "Very Warm for May" *bombed* on Broadway; however, a few years later Oklahoma! hit Broadway like a *bombshell."* (*Contronym* seems to be a word not yet recognized by dictionaries. – Ed)

Cutlines, the fouled-up kind: What happened in a cutline (PP, 11-9) didn't tell us very much about the photo just above it. The photo seemed to show St. Paul Mayor Randy Kelly delivering his concession speech and consisted of two rows of the same word: *cutline cutline cutline cutline...* 26 times. It could have been much worse. A celebrated cutline foulup by the Chicago Tribune, a long time ago, contained two adjacent photos: one of a prominent dowager, the other a building about to be demolished. Under the woman's photo was a sub-head with the words "Old Landmark Passes." It goes with the territory. "He that is without sin among you, let him cast a stone...")

Fads: *Parameter*: "Both projects are within the market *parameters...*" (ST edit, 9-29). "[Its use] suggests that the writer has not understood the technical sense and has chosen it primarily as a way of injecting an aura of scientific precision into what would otherwide be a pedestrian communication... difficulties appear to arise from its resemblance to *perimeter,* with which it shares the meaning of 'limit.'" (AHD) Wördo Prof. Ray Warner: *"Parameter* in mathematics means 'a variable that is temporarily held constant.'" Sixty-two percent of AHD's Usage Panel disapproves of using the word in the sense of "limits."

Huh? "Missing Student's Autopsy Complete" (head, ST, 9-29). Autopsy on a missing student? "Both are 52 years old," (John Reger, WCCO-TV News, 10-9). About a couple that had been murdered. No, John. They aren't *52*, they were 52. "...an area *hardly* hit..." (CNN, 9-24, re New Orleans). Contradiction between *hardly* and *hard!* "They would *ferment* (foment) unrest," (Bill O'Reilly, Ch60 Fox TV, 9-28). "The essential criteria (criterion) is..." (Brian Lambert, The Rake, Oct. issue). "Enjoy time on your private patio or in your garage," (Ad for town home, Owatonna P-P, 10-16). YFIO *"Legend has it* he received a recommendation..." (Patrick Reusse, ST, 10-11). Rumor. In a story about a drug test, a CBS announcer referred to "dummy pills" instead of *placebos.* Wördo Fred Webber: "Must have thought no one knows what a placebo is." "Driver *Charged Deaths* of 23 Killed In Bus Fire" (ST, 10-18). Missing preposition: *In* deaths. "...*missing person's name here*" (Minn. Newspaper Foundation promo piece, undtd.). "(They are) bound not to talk to anyone *accept* other cardinals," (Seattle Times, 4-17).

Typos – the *now-not* confusion: Spelling *now* when *not* is intended can give a contrary meaning to the sentence. "To the prosecutor... they're serious crimes that are prosecuted 'all the time,' but that's *now* (not!) how Washington veterans view them. It all depends who's accused of the crimes," (NYT, 11-1). "...Seven Dwarfs *diddy* (ditty) and *souzaphone* (sousaphone)," (ST, 10-5).

Punctuation – the ironic use of quotation marks: "George W. Bush *'won'* that remarkable *'election'* in 2000," (Molly Ivins, ST, 10-19). A perfect example of quotes used to convey irony. What Ms. Ivins means by using those quotes is that George Bush really didn't win, and it wasn't an honest-to-goodness election. A large, temporary sign without an apostrophe: "WERE DEALING" near Le Sueur this summer, could have been read: "We were dealing, but not any more." (Thanks, Stringer Craig Kotasek, Gaylord Hub)

Spelling trauma: Wördo Helen Beggs: "While Frank Vascellaro talked about banks *waiving* mortgage payments for victims of Katrina, the wording on the screen behind him read *Mortgages Waved*," (CH11, 9-9). "Education officials saw the *whole* (hole) and should be congratulated for filling it," (Lakeshore Wkly News, 9-27). "I buy *property's*," (same, ad, 10-11). "...we'll be *alright*" (Exc.-Shorewood Sun-Sailor, 9-22).

— yr humble & obt svt, Robert M. Shaw.

WÖRDOS

The English language super sleuths.

March 18, 2007

Wördos? About 20 persons, mostly retired teachers or journalists, who meet once a month in Minneapolis and talk about our English language. Abbreviations: ST = Minneapolis Star Tribune, PP = St. Paul Pioneer Press, NYT = N.Y.Times, WSJ = Wall St. Journal, unatt = don't know source, undtd = don't know date, UM = unidentified miscreant, AHD = Am. Heritage Dict. III, GMAU = Garner's Mod. Am. Usage, OED = Oxford Dict. Of Eng. Lang. II, YFIO = you figure it out. Italics used freely for emphasis. Contributions welcome! We have a Web page: *http://www.Wördos.net.* We also have a high-falutin' motto, supplied by Classicist Jeremiah Reedy: *Claritas super omnia:* clarity above all!

Detours

"Nothing like that has ever happened in the *anals* (annals) of history!" Stringer Pete Sneve swears he heard this on KBJR-TV (Duluth-Superior) on Feb. 28. The problem lay in the pronunciation of *annals*, Sneve said. (Thanks, Charlie Johnson.)

> *"A former forklift truck,* Steven Wright, was found guilty
> of murdering five prostitutes in Ipswich." (NYT, 2-22)

"They were married on Feb. 2, 1925, when Mayme was
16 years old, *and had six children.*" (ST, 2-18)

"Troy Williams ... hasn't lived up to the expectations *as
expected of him.*" (Sid Hartman, ST, 2-17)

"While working in the flower garden last Thursday, Mrs. Johnson
bent over to pick a lucky four-leaf clover as a bumblebee flew up her
dress and stung her on the." (Van Buren [Ark.] Press Argus, undtd.,
from Press Boners, Earle Tempel.)

Agreement, dis-: *"Here's* (here are) 10 things to monitor." (ST, 2-18)
"Judges are scratching *their head* (heads)." (Time, undtd) "Tunes In Our
Head (heads)" (AARP mag, 1-2) "A series of gunshots *were* (was) heard."
(ST, 1-16) "... a stand of trees that *were* (was) marked for removal."
(newsltr, Plymouth News, undtd)

Apostrophes, lack: "Israeli leaders have long imagined ... *Jordan*
(Jordan's) taking control." (ST, 1-25) "Payments could begin flowing
'within 60 days' of *Bush* (Bush's) signing..." (ST, 1-25) "(The case)
led to the *U.S. Supreme Court* (Court's) banning execution of the
mentally retarded." (ST, 1-19) "... higher rating than any other *candidate*
(candidate's)." (David Brook, NYT, 2-24) "And McCain will not long
be amused by *Huckabee* (Huckbee's) continuing to offer himself as a
(conservative) vessel." (ST, 2-24)

Bravos! Bright metaphors! Paul Levy, in a ST 1-18 piece, brightened
a story about high-speed rail with several metaphors taken from the
fields of gambling and railroading. The story related to construction of a
railroad to Duluth, and is much favored by Grand Casino, at Hinckley.
"On the same track" (re comparison of costs), "(the federals) *control the
switch,* everyone is expected to *remain on board"* (re a TEMS study),
"some *high-speed glitches"* (re funding), "The *engine driving that line"*
(a comparable project in Maine), "proponents are *betting on* Grand

Casino" (which loves the project), and "the Mille Lacs Band is *taking a back seat* from no one."

More bright ones: "(His campaign) seems sad – sputtering, stalling and dying like a bad engine on an old car." (NYT, 1-27) "Wine is a mocker, strong drink a brawler." (King James Bible, Proverbs 10.1) "(Hope that Ohio and Texas) will *provide a seawall* against the Obama surge." (NYT, 2-13) "A *poisonous spiral* of economic stress and cultural decay." (David Brooks, NYT, 2-15)

Right words! "Court *Quashes* Terror Convictions" (ST head, 2-14) "*Quash*: To set aside or annul." "Consumers are *short-shrifted.*" (David Phelps, ST, 2-14. "*Short shrift:* summary, careless treatment, scant attention." AHD)

Graduate, as transitive verb: "Only 35 percent of Baltimore students *graduate high school* within four years." (Col. Journalism Rev., 1-2) No: "The transitive use of *graduate,* as in *She graduated Yale in 1980,* is unacceptable to 77 percent of the Usage Panel." (AHD)

Huh? "You shoot into the woods and hope you get a *game.*" (Wis. sheriff on WCCO-News, 10-27) "The parents of those killed *must have been taken aback.*" (Sheriff quote, NBC News, 10-28) "... the economy *shrunk* (shrank) in 23 states." (NYT, 2-23) "The terrible *rally* (volley?) of gunfire ..." (ST head, 2-15) "He was sent *to a troubled home* for teens." (CH5, 2-16. No. A home for troubled teens.) "(He) helped her to bill due dates to *jive* (jibe) with her paychecks." (Joe Pitzi, ST, 1-18)." "Pleasing Works *On Displayed* at Neilson Place." (Bemidji Pioneer, 1-15)

Likes of, two divergent meanings. Derogatory: "... politically charged attacks *by the likes of* Joe Kennedy and Mark Montigny." (GMAU). But also positive, praiseworthy: "Gathering *the likes of* Henry Kissinger and Margaret Thatcher ..." (NYT, 7-14) "...ring in the new year with a fireworks show *the likes of* which nobody's seen for a century." (GMAU) "*The likes of* Ben Franklin, George Washington, John Jay, Washington

Irving (who) took their places as authorities." ("Word Wizard," Richard Lederer)

Cliches banished because of "misuse, overuse, and general uselessness:" (From Lake Superior St. University, Sault Ste. Marie) "Warm, fuzzy feeling," "my plate is full," "read my lips," "been there, done that," "cautiously optimistic," "don't even go there" and "happy camper." Also listed: armed gunman, completely destroy, totally demolish, hunker down, untimely death, capture alive, sworn affidavit, senseless murder, the bottom line, creative utterances, wakeup call, the race card, no-brainer, networking, do-able, done deal, downsizing, level playing field, downsizing, faith based, quality time, sea change, tough row to hoe, and upscale. "Cliches are a sad subject, really, always reminding us of the repetitiveness of things, the humdrumness that lies beyond and within the doorstep if one's imagination should weaken or one's sense of humour runs out." (R. W. Burchfield, Fowler's Modern English Usage.)

Spelling goofs: *Egoist* and *egotist,* apparently, are both acceptable spellings with AHD. "Doesn't *phase* (faze) Ashraf..." (Owatonna PP, 11-18) "...*there* (their) convention." (PP, 7-22) "... and the stores that sell their *wears* (wares)." (PP, undtd) "...*unchartered* (uncharted) territory." (Fillmore Co. Jnl, 9-17) "...hunters compete over their favorite bear *sight* (site)." (MN Conservation Officer Tales, Sept. nsltr) "It threatens to *undue* (undo) the good things." (D. Brooks, NYT, 2-5) "*Slyder* burgers. (Sold by White Castle. Deliberately misspelled.)

Words, good ones, worthy of review: *Reprise,* as in "...urged Mr. Edwards to *reprise* his theme." (NYT, 11-23) "A phrase that has been bitterly *reprised* by Democrats." (New Yorker mag, 1-28 "*Reprise:* return to an original theme.") **Wonky**, as in "Mrs. Clinton's combative, *wonky* incrementalism." (NYT, 2-3) "*Wonky:* shaky, feeble, awry.) **Thwart**, as in "...that would neatly *thwart* the party-vetting process." (NYT, 2-15. "*Thwart:* To prevent the occurrence of." **Coalesce:** as in "the party should begin *coalescing* around him." (NYT, 2-20. "*Coalesce:* To grow together, to fuse." "***Scofflaw:*** One who habitually violates the law." ***Seed,*** as in "The simplest approach would be to *seed* universal mutual fund accounts for low-income Americans." (NYT, 2-22. "*Seed:* To arrange the drawings for positions in a tournament so that the more skilled contestants meet in the later rounds. AHD for all entries.)

Words seen for the first time: Merriam Webster's Word of the Year is ***w00t,*** a combination of letters and numbers. It's used by gamesters to express great happiness. ***Millenarion***, as in "Google's projects have elicited *millenarion* prophesies." (New Yorker mag, 11-5. Still searching.) ***Snark,*** as in "The feature is lame but the premise is *snark.*" (NYT, 10-22. *Snark,* in Random House Coll. Dict: "A creature imagined by Lewis Carroll, part snail and part shark." But as an adjective? YFIO) - yr humble & obt svt, Robert MacGregor Shaw.

WÖRDOS

The English language super sleuths.

May 22, 2007

(Wördos? A group of about 20 persons, most of them retired, who get together to talk about words, chiefly words that take a beating in the media. Most Wördos were teachers or journalists. Abbreviations, to save space: ST = Minneapolis Star Tribune, PP = St. Paul Pioneer Press, NYT = N.Y.Times; WSJ = Wall St. Journal, unatt = don't know source, undtd = don't know date; AHD = Am. Heritage Dictionary III, GMAU = Garner's Modern Am. Usage, OED = Oxford Dict. Of Eng. Lang. II, YFIO = you figure it out, UM = unidentified miscreant, re = regarding. Visit our website: www.Wördos.net. Contributions welcome! – Ed.)

Early Weeds

(Concerning a 3-25 spay-neuter clinic in Rochester:) **"It attracted cats *and their owners* from throughout southeastern Minnesota."** (Rochester P-B., 3-26. Two for the price of one. Covered by Medicare?) **"A motion was made ... to have Pro Landscaping *pray for weeds."*** (Gaylord Hub, 5-9. Good for business! Thanks, Hub-Ed Jim Deis!) **"(Denver has a ban on pit bulls) forcing owners to *turn the animals into authorities."*** (Seattle Times, 7-21-'05) "Side effects may include ***drowziness."*** (TV ad for sleeping pill, unatt.-undtd. Their spelling, too.) "Nokomis Roofing, *literally covering the entire metro area."* (KTNF-AM, 3-20. Literally died laughing.)

Lexicographers struggle with a nonsense word

The 19th century English mathematician and writer Charles Lutwidge Dodgson (1832-1898), a.k.a Lewis Carroll, wrote a nonsense poem, "Jabberwocky" that has long been of interest to linguists. It's filled with nonsense words that sound like everyday words we know: a *beamish boy* takes his *vorpal* sword in hand and kills a *frumious Jabberwock* which comes *galumphing* through the *tulgey* wood *and "...burbled* as it came." Wördo Marlene Reuber checked out *galumphing* and reports that lexicographers have supplied definitions. Marlene: "The Free Online Dictionary says it means 'To move or run clumsily or heavily.' Dictionary. com agrees and goes on to explain that it is a 'phonesthemic invention of Lewis Carroll, perhaps a combination of *gallop* and *triumph.'* Webster's Second claims that *galumph* means 'to march or prance along in a self-satisfied, triumphant manner.'" OED II, daddy dictionary of them all, also cites *galumph:* "To march off exultantly with irregular, bounding movements... now, usu., to bound or move clumsily or noisily." Lewis Carroll unfortunately is not around to tell us what he, inventor of the word, intended it to mean.

★   ★   ★   ★

Apt words, phrases: "You can't invite a guest of honor to come and be a political *piñata,"* (Steve Scully, C-SPAN, re annual D.C. Correspondents' Ass'n. dinner). "On Lake Ice, Beware The *Carp Pool"* (ST head, 2-22, re shallow areas favored by carp in Minneapolis's lakes).

Huh? "Microwave butter at full power *for 60 to 90 minutes* until melted," (Mary Hunt, P-P, undtd.). The microwave melted, too. "The house *sits* (rests?) on city property," (Plainview News, 4-12). "Sunday, March (blank!), 2007, Section G," (ST, undtd). "The task force was *headed up* by Mike Carlson," (ST, 2-27). Wördo Fred Webber: "Why *up?* Why not *headed by?"* "In *Them Days,* Snowthrowers Were Snowthrowers," (ST head, undtd). Copy-editor assumed reader would understand facetious use of *"them days.""*Be A Pal, Al, *Leave* Us Be," (ST, 3-1). Again, playful use of *leave.* But could be understood as an error.

Healthy-healthful: The distinction between *healthy* (robust) and *healthful* (conducive to health) is certainly being lost. "...another form of *unhealthy* expression," (Grand Forks Herald, 10-26-'06). Somehow we need a better adjective. "The joy of *healthy* (healthful) cooking," (Exp. Life, 10-'06). "...*healthy* eating," (Owatonna PP, 7-14).

Laser-lase: "Labels Could Soon Be *Lasered On* To Fruit," (Winona Dly News, undtd). OED II: *"Lase:* Back formation from *laser*... to operate as a laser." Dictionaries haven't caught up with this one. LASER, by the way = Light Amplification by Stimulated Radiation.

Lie – lay – laid – lain: "She *laid* (LAY) back down," (Chao Xiong, ST, 11-28). Wördo Fred Webber noticed that *laid* was changed to *lay* in the online version. "...he was *laying* (LYING) on the sidewalk," (John Mason, CH5, 11-22-'06). "...found his wife *laying* (LYING) on the dock," (Mille Lacs Messenger, 3-14). "...as the man *laid* (LAY) on the ground," (Rochelle Olson, ST, 2-13). "...as the man *laid* (LAY) on the ground," (Rochelle Olson, ST, 2-13). This, unatt. wisdom: "The proper word for the reclining position, *lying*, was enforced by propriety. Speakers were careful not to besmirch others with the shameful sexual innuendo, *laying*. There is no longer any shame in sex, whereas there is shame, at least in principle, in *lying*."

Metaphors, good ones: Wördo Ray Warner, a retired professor of electrical engineering: "The ladder analogy is a highly valid metaphor for understanding the nature of mathematics. Every time you ascend to another rung (arithmetic, geometry, analytic geometry, calculus, et. al.,) you acquire a better understanding of the one(s) before." "Chuck Hagel is a caribou among Holsteins," (Garrison Keillor, NYT, 2-11). "(Talk show) trolls go berserk in their webby caverns whenever she (Hillary Clinton) comes trotting over the bridge," (Maureen Dowd, NYT, 2-11).
Mixed metaphors: "I went in to a small lake... one last visit in the snow before *winter's grip had melted,"* (Kevin Proescholdt, ST, undtd).

Pronunciation: Wördo Maryjane Reagan heard Sen. Zell Miller of Georgia pronounce *electoral* with an extra syllable: "Ee-lec- tor-EE-al," (undtd). Wördo Ray Warner: "When speaking the number 243, one should say 'Two hundred forty-three,' rather than two hundred *and* forty three. The *and* designates a decimal point. Just because I'm paranoid doesn't mean you're not out to get me," he says. Feb-YEW-ary (CH4, 2-10) as opposed to Feb-RU-ary, seems to be gaining ground.

Punctuation: "...they were to discuss the possibility of *Poland* (Poland's) serving as a hub," (ST, 9-14). "A close friend of *Diana's...*" (ST, 12-15-'06). Close friend of Diana, or just Diana's friend. "...intervening in other *nation's* (nations') affairs," (NYT, 2-10). "Proper punctuation is both the sign and the cause of clear thinking," ("Eats, Shoots and Leaves," Truss, 2003).

Spelling – typo or ignorance? "...ready to take the *reigns,*" (Ctr. For Rural Affairs nsltr, undtd). "...*reign* in *mortgage lending,*" (PP, 1-19). "*Your* (you're) invited," (Owatonna P-P, 1-27).

Time – moving it up, moving it back: "Stores *moved up* their post-Thanksgiving opening times..." (Sara Glassman, ST, 11-25, '06). The store normally opened at 5 p.m.; it changed to a later hour of 9 p.m. Wördos claim this is correct! "The launch was *pushed back...* to late April," (ST, 2-28). NO! It was pushed ahead, postponed, advanced!

Unique "(It was) *most unique,*" (Pat Evans, CH11, 11-17-'06). No. *Unique* can't be qualified. GMAU: "*Unique* means 'being one of a kind,' not 'unusual.' The phrases *very unique, quite unique, how unique* are slovenly." "...somewhat *unique,*" (Anthony Lonetree, ST, 2-11).

Words we've seen for the first time: *Clawbacks,* as in "All deals should include *clawbacks,*" (ST, 5-6). ***Hoovered up,*** as a verb in "...visas are being *hoovered up,*" (Time, 4-9). No sign of it in three dictionaries. OED: "*Hoover*: To clean with a Hoover (or by extension any) vacuum cleaner." Also: "*Hooverize:* to be sparing or economical, especially in the use of food." ***Ombudsmandry***, as in "…the fascinating field of *ombudsmandry*," (Kate Parry, ST, 4-15). No can find. ***Impactful:*** "It's more *impactful*," (Quote, Twins Promo Dir., 9-5-'06). Can't locate. ***Pluripotentiality:*** "They (amniotic cells) show great *pluripotentiality*," (Unatt., meaning they can make many kinds of tissues. No sign of it in AHD).

You figure it out: "Lukan said the basic *pretense* (pretext? precept?) of internet hunting is offensive," (AP, Outdoor News, 3-9). "My dad… *cemented his contention* that it was best to pick a good spot," (Minn. Outdoor News, 3-9). "You and I have a lot of common beliefs that are the same and we have some that are different," (Quote, Rudy Giuliani, ST, 3-3). And we have some that are the same and different at the very same time. "Minnesota's house of the future will have no carbon emissions, meaning it will need no fossil fuels," (ST, 3-25). Sounds bass-ackwards.

— yr humble & obt svt, Robert MacGregor Shaw

WÖRDOS

The English language super sleuths.

June 19, 2007

(Wördos? A group of about 20 persons, most of them retired, who get together to talk about words, chiefly words that take a beating in the media. Most Wördos were teachers or journalists. Abbreviations, to save space: ST = Minneapolis Star Tribune, PP = St. Paul Pioneer Press, NYT = N.Y.Times; WSJ = Wall St. Journal, unatt = don't know source, undtd = don't know date; AHD = Am. Heritage Dictionary III, GMAU = Garner's Modern Am. Usage, OED = Oxford Dict. Of Eng. Lang. II, YFIO = you figure it out, UM = unidentified miscreant, re = regarding. Visit our website: www.Wördos.net. Contributions welcome! – Ed.)

Road bumps

"There are clouds behind that silver lining," (Gwen Ifel, CH2, 4-27).
"(It's) the *backside of the front,*" (Weatherman, WCCO, 4-10).
"Verna D. Korman, age 98, died April 14, 2007... was
preceded in death by her parents," (Owatonna P-P, 4-14).
"Top Secret Sandwich Recipe: (2 egg yolks, 1 slice bread, etc.)
and *8 to 12 cups vegetable shortening,*" (Oh, yuck-k-k!).

Runner-up for all-time goofs

"(The poet has had) three works of poetry published in an anthology entitled 'Paper Sailors,' a *copulation* of work from the Women's Guild of Central Florida," (Washburn, Wis., County Journal, undtd).

"The healing evangelist... *wore a black suit, which he removed* after the sermon and before the healing began," (Clark Morphew, PP, 3-22-'97).

Ambiguous reference: Whenever a pronoun is used, its antecedent should be clear to the reader. Ambiguous: "When Jim attacked George, he was very angry." (Jim or George?) "There's a fly in your salad. Want to eat it?" (Salad or fly?) "A pedestrian was hit by a car crossing the street." (Was the car crossing or was the pedestrian?) (Post Bulletin, an Internet grammar column.) "...they were lying next to the three when they were shot in the head and ran to get help after the gunman left," (PP, 3-27). This says they were shot in the head and then ran for help. "A study reveals that girls are more likely to abuse prescription drugs *than boys,*" (John Mason, CH5, 5-1). So: Girls would rather abuse prescription drugs than abuse boys. "*Based on* their findings, researchers estimated that..." (ST, undtd). This says that researchers were based on findings. "(A Hastings man) led authorities on a nine-mile chase early Wednesday, during which he dragged a sheriff's deputy with his vehicle as he tried to flee?" (Tim Harlow, ST, 5-3). Wördo Fred Webber: "Whose vehicle? Who tried to flee?"

Causes, lost ones: *Unique:* "This material is *a little bit unique,*" (Reporter, CH11, 1-12-'07). "*Most Unique* Western Store in Minnesota" (I-35 sign, Owatonna). Too many unique-goof cites to list here. *Unique* can't be qualified! ***Healthy-healthful:*** "...*healthy* (HEALTHFUL!), nutritious foods," (ST, undtd). "*Healthy* (HEALTHFUL!) options," (ST, undtd). "If my lunch were *healthy,* it would still be swimming somewhere," (Joy Wiltius, Fort Collins, Colo., Lake Sup. U. bulletin). The distinction between *healthy* (robust) and *healthful* (conducive to health) surely is on its way out.

Fads: *Awesome:* The word was banished by Lake Superior State U.'s 2007 List of Banished Words: "...it will not be rehabilitated until it means 'fear mingled with admiration or reverence; a feeling produced by something majestic,'" (LSSU bulletin). **Went missing**: "This makes 'missing' sound like a place you can visit, such as the Poconos. Is the person missing, or not? She went there, but maybe she came back," (Robin Dennis, Flower Mound, Tex., LSSU bull.). **Truthiness** seems to be on its way out. It was Am. Dialectic Soc.'s Word of 2005.

Guns, banning of: "ATK Bans Guns In Our Facility," (Sign on the door of ATK, a company that makes missiles, bombs, strike weapons, fuses, and ammunition. Spotted by Stringer Bill Farmer, 3-9).

Huh? "His grammar was *network perfect!*" (c.j. [sic] col., ST, 4-22). "He was very bi-partisan *on both sides,*" (Legislator, NPR Almanac, 4-27). "At Least 9 Dead After Kan. Tornado" (Owatonna PP, 5-6). Maybe more, they think. "Couples plan to start marriages on a *fortuitous* foot," (Ad, PP, 4-10). *Fortuitous:* Happening by accident or chance," AHD. "I was raised here... I know it *intricately* (intimately?) (PP quote, 3-4). "Vicious *Cycle* (Circle) Rolls On" (ST head, 4-19). "...the other *four* (five, in the copy) lakes..." (ST cutline, undtd). "The Cardinals need a left tackle and they *won't care to reach for one,*" (ST, 4-28). YFIO. "Rub Don't Blot!" Wördo Ray Warner: "It was common for a paper-towel dispenser to carry that suggestion embossed into the metal. Someone, though, wrote firmly below: 'If rub don't blot, why should we?'" "Some companies would *loan* (lend) you a copy machine." (New Yorker, 3-19)

Quotes, ironic: "(The board cited Wolfowitz's) "good faith" on the ethics issue," (NYT, 5-18). The problem here is that the quotes around *good faith* may be interpreted in two ways. To the writer, they meant accuracy: those were the board's very words. To the reader, the quotes may mean that the writer signals that he questions Wolfowitz's "good faith" and uses quotes to express skepticism. "Dallas Sams, 54, *'Beloved'* Senator," (PP head, 3-6). An innocent reader might conclude the writer believed Sen. Sams was a scumbag.

> ### Noun phrase, clunking into over-use
> *From an essay in Verbatim, The Language Quarterly.*
>
> "Have you heard a new 'clunk-clunk' sound in the English language? Phrases such as 'patient starter package' for sample? 'Drug dosage forms' for pills? 'Health cause' for sickness. 'Increased labor market participation rates' for more people working? ... I've dubbed this phenomenon 'Nounspeak' in allusion to 'Newspeak' about which Orwell wrote: 'Newspeak is designed not to extend but to diminish the range of thought.'
>
> "We daily encounter excrescences like 'growth trend pattern' and 'consumer price inflation' and even, hold your hat, 'U.S.Air Force aircraft fuel systems equipment mechanics course.' People aren't broke any more. They have a money problem or a bad money situation. Weathermen don't predict rain any more: now it's precipitation activity.
>
> "People often have the sensation that they aren't being heard. So they keep lumping noun on noun, as though by saying the same thing two or three times, they'll be understood across the existential void. It's reasonable to ask that our writers and editors steer us away from Nounspeak's worst excesses. We'll know the tide has turned when the IRS whittles its Tax Schedule Rate Chart down to Tax Rate Chart, then to the very sensible Tax Chart, then – unlikely victory – to Taxes, which is what they were trying to say all along." (Thanks to Wördo Jeremiah Reedy for spotting this one. —Ed.)

Troops: It's PLURAL – may not be used to indicate a single soldier. It's also degrading. This, from Patricia Juaire of Roseville (letter, PP, 2-4): "To say '23 *troops* were killed in Iraq over the weekend' dehumanizes and distracts... I am sure that the families of those injured or killed do not think of their loved one as a 'troop.' Let's at least name them sons or daughters, husbands or wives, even dads and moms: real people."

Outdoor-outdoors: There's a difference: *Outdoor:* Located, done, or suited to the open air. *Outdoors:* Outside. In or into the open; anywhere away from human settlements," (Both, AHD). "The sales tax for *outdoors* (outdoor) and cultural programs," (ST, undtd).

Stringer report: Stringer Wally Allen, former associate executive editor of the Minneapolis Tribune, now retired in Honolulu: "All of a sudden I repeatedly see the expression *having said that* in the local press. The phrase has no referent. Nobody has said anything. It's like a nervous tic. Have you detected this virus on the mainland?"

Words, loathful: *Fun*, as an adjective: "BMW – '97-Z3, 2-dr. convt, 5 spd., silver, *very fun...*" (Winona Daily News, 5-9). ***Undocumented alien***: "If they haven't followed the law to get in, they are by definition *illegal*. It's like saying a drug dealer is an 'undocumented pharmacist,'" (John Varga, Westfield, N.J. LSSU bull.). ***Launch***, as in "We then *launched* a more intensive investigation," (NYT quote, 3-11). Has always sounded too pretentious. – Ed.

Words, good ones, seldom used: *Ethos,* as in "a folksy, country *ethos,*" (NYT, 6-1). *"Ethos:* Fundamental character or value specific to a specific person, people, culture or movement," (AHD). ***Devolution,*** as "the *devolution* of power," (NYT, 6-5). ***"Devolution:*** A passing down or descent through successive stages of time... devolution of authority or duties... a transfer of power," (AHD). ***Scion:*** descendent, heir. Pronounced "SIGH-on." ***Quotidian,*** as in "quotidian tapes," (Time, 3-5). *"Quotidian:* everyday, commonplace," AHD.

Words seen for the first time: *Aspirational,* as in "The environmental goals are *aspirational,*" (James Connaughton, advisor to Pres. Bush, NYT, 6-1). ***Commoditization,*** as in "...what some would call the *commoditization* of our brand," (Starbucks exec. quote, PP, 2-24). YFIO. ***Determinately*** as in "He has worked *determinately* (deterministically, AHD) to prevent predators from attacking our children," (ST, 4-22).

— yr humble & obt svt, Robert MacGregor Shaw

WÖRDOS

The English language super sleuths.

Contributions are welcome! Send to: Bob Shaw, 6216 Oriole Lane, Edina, MN 55436, 952-927-5208 Visit our website at www.Wördos.net

August 15, 2006

Wördos? A loose organization of friends who like to meet and talk about words. Well, not just talk; argue, dispute. *Logomachy:* (AHD) "A dispute carried on in words only." Abbreviations: ST = Mpls Star Tribune, PP = St. Paul Pioneer-Press, NYT = New York Times, WSJ = Wall St. Jnl., OED = Oxford Dictionary of English Lang., AHD = American Heritage Dictionary III, WEG = Warriner's Eng. Grammar & Composition, YFIO = you figure it out. Italics used freely for emphasis. unatt = don't know source, undtd = don't know date, re = regarding, head = headline. All entries contributed by Wördos, all dates 2006's unless flagged. Contributions welcome! The umlaut in Wördos commemorates our founder, Bjorn Bjornson. For more information, visit our website: www.Wördos.net

Screeching stops

"If you or a loved one have had a stroke, a blood clot *or
died* after using Ortho Evra, call Peterson & Associates,"
(ST ad, 6-21). Died. Can't call, but thanks anyway.
"A... restaurant in Chatfield was *armed at gunpoint*
late Friday evening," (Rochester P-B, 7-10).
"Cooper could face life in prison *without parole or death*," (PP, 2-3).

★   ★   ★   ★

Agreement, lack of: "...asked Mozart to compose for *he* (HIM) and his daughter," (Steve Staruch, MPR, 6-19). "Between *he* (HIM) and his competitor," (Larry Smith, CNN, 2-19). "...prosecutors *which* (WHO) accused him," (unatt, 3-3). "*Bacteria* that *has* (HAVE) infected his knee," (Time, 6-26). It's plural. "...turmoil among (between) *he* (HIM) and his partners," (Graydon Royce, ST, 5-13). "One in eight babies *are* (IS)..." (Rochester P-B, 7-14). "A task force... *have* (HAS) spread..." (ST, 5-20).

Ambiguous reference: "Anyone caught operating *while intoxicated by a village officer* will pay," (Burnett Co. [Wis] Sentinel, 3-15). Sneaky. "...officials are expected to charge him with fondling the young girls *as early as tomorrow.*" (Mark Albert, CH5 News, 7-3). Fondler has set the time and place; cops will be there to observe.

Defuse-diffuse: "Most sides were looking for ways to *diffuse* the situation," (ST, undated). "Trying to *defuse* the crisis..." (ST, 7-16). Wördo Ray Warner observes that both words are being used to describe efforts to quell violence in the Middle East. *Defuse* means to remove the ignition from an explosive device; *diffuse* means to spread or disperse. It seems that *defuse* in this context is more appropriate.

Fads – look to, and push back: (AHD) "*Fad:* A fashion that is taken up with great enthusiasm for a brief amount of time. A craze." ***Look to:*** "Washington County *Looks To* Add Deputies" (ST, 7-16). First *look to* seen in a long time. ***Push back:*** "...they agreed to *push back* the date," (PP, 2-4) and "...*pushing back* the trial date," (PP, 2-20). They did not push it back. They postponed it, set it ahead. "Three meetings have been *pushed back* (NO! Postponed!) in order to allow more time..." (PP, 11-30-'05). ***Pushed up:*** "Initially (the event) was supposed to start in fall 2005. Then it was *pushed up* to this year," (PP, 4-19). Advanced? Postponed? Re-scheduled? Re-set? If you can push a date up, can you also push it down?

First annual: "...*first annual* chicken dinner and dance will be held ...Saturday," (Burnet County [Wis] Sentinel, 6-7). Can't be *first annual* until one year after the initial chicken dinner and dance.

Hate words & phrases: Wördo Ray Warner: ***Sharing a common view.*** Jonah Goldberg (ST, 6-24) writes, "In the phrase 'media *share a common view,*' let it be *media share a view* or else *media hold a common view.*" Warner also has a strong dislike to the phrase **broader point,** as in "Our *broader point* is that..." (ST edit, 7-13). A point that's broadened, Warner says, is no longer a point. Wördo Fred Webber is bothered by **graduated high school, as in** "Forty-four percent of Minnesota's black students *graduated high school,*" (ST, 7-19). Webber: "This, from Richard Lederer: '*Graduated high school* is coming in, and it may be standard one day, just as *I graduated from* superseded *I was graduated from,* but not yet.'"

Healthy-healthful: "On Having *Healthful* (healthy) Employees" (ST head, 11-6-'05). "*Healthy* (Healthful) Food Choices" (Blake School Cafeteria). "*Healthier* (more healthful) Hospital Food" (Time, 5-22). *Healthful:* conducive to health. *Healthy:* robust. The distinction between these two words is surely disappearing.

Huh? "Edisher Savitski, a burly 29-year-old pianist born in Tbilisi, Georgia, was named winner Thursday night ...at Orchestra Hall," (Michael Anthony, ST, 7-14). Tbilisi's just south of Atlanta. Edisher's a southern boy. "*Grant it* (granted), a lot were friends," (Burnett

[Wis.] Co. Sentinel, 3-15). "It was *cut and dry,*" (Commonwealth, Feb. issue). "Norway has ...established a high standard, *advocating for* (NO! Advocating!) environmental sustainability," (ST, 6-23). "...*sites* (sights) set on additional stores," (Lake M'tonka Navigator, July). "(Signers of the Declaration) would have been *hung* (hanged) if they were caught," (USA Weekend, 7-30). "Relief (for Ford Plant workers) Is Short-Lived; 'It's Still In *Purgatory*'" and "Workers *In Limbo* As Union Works To Spare Plant" (Head and sub-head, PP, 1-24). AHD: *"Limbo: The abode of just or innocent souls excluded from the beatific vision but not condemned for further punishment... one of the words to refer to oblivion, confinement, or transition." From Latin *limbus:* border.

Hyphenate? "...Halloween *make-up* (makeup?)" (Rochester P-B, 6-25). "Albright... could *leg press* (leg-press?) 400 pounds," (ST, 5-25).

Lie-lay: "Did you ever have an MRI *laying* (LYING) down?" (KSTP-FM Radio, 4-28, ad for Life Scan MRI). Do they give them standing up? "Small Boy *Laying* Down" (Ad, Marshall Fields, Ridgedale, undt, unatt.). "Her body *laying* (lying) 12 feet below the water," and "He must have *laid* (lain) there up to an hour," (Both, John Quinois (sp?) ABC Primetime, 6-22). "I'm gonna spend my summer *laying* (lying) out on the patio," (ST, 6-4, Sally Forth comic).

Preposition problems: "Stop *into* (in) one of our stores," (CH5 ad, 6-29). "Meetings of which I was not a partner in," (Pres. Bush's press sec'y., 7-5). "A division *based out of* Iraq," (CH5, 6-14). "...counsel can benefit *from* (by) becoming familiar with its ...jurisprudence," (Bench & Bar, April).

Truthiness – new word: It was coined by Stephen Colbert, Producer of The Colbert Report, a satirical mock news show on the Comedy Channel. "Truthiness" has been defined as quality by which a person purports to know something intuitively or instinctively without regard to evidence. The word *truthy* is defined by the OED as a "variation of straightforward truthfulness." *Truthiness* was selected as Word of the

Year by the American Dialect Society, and by the NYT as one of nine words that captured the spirit of 2005. The word should be enclosed in quotes: "Use quotation marks to enclose slang words, technical terms, and other expressions that are unusual in standard English." (WEG)

TV people doing their bit: "Neither *were* (WAS) charged," (Mark Daley, CH11, 3-22). "A talent only one in 100,000 *have* (has)," (Leslie Stahl, 60 Minutes, 6-25). "The risk of rain is *nil and void*," (Weatherman, CH5, 7-4). "They have been and will continue to stand by," (WCCO News, 5-29). "The man was *beaten and attacked*," (CH5, 6-15). But not in that order. "...that's not *set in stone*," (Jud Zulgad, ST, 6-2). One carves in stone, sets in concrete. "The fact that they were able to do this should be illegal," (CH2, 5-23). Illegal facts.

YFIO: You Figure It Out: "...he was frequently *skipping out of school*," (David Chanen, ST, 4-13). "He could ultimately quit his job and just move on. Or he may not have gone at all." ... "I'm not *advocating people* to vote for someone based on my political philosophy," (Both, Burnett [Wis.] Co. Sentinel, 3-15). "The task force started by *complying* with the facts," (Lakeshore Wkly News, 7-4). "The observatory (is located) in *Baker* Park... and *Baylor* Park," (same piece, ST, 6-21). "Like many of New *Orleans* (Orleans's) neighborhoods, Katrina destroyed his home," (CBS, 5-20). This says that Katrina is a neighborhood. "...a war-torn Marine," (CH5, 6-8). "(Re a parked car) ...nobody knew who *put it* (left it? parked it? abandoned it?) there," (ST, 6-2). Wördo Fred Webber: "Sounds as though somebody lowered it on a crane." "*Prejudism:*" (Wördo Bill Farrell swears he heard somebody say that brand-new word on KFAN Radio, 2-19.)

— yr humble & obt svt, Robert MacGregor Shaw

Word from the Wördos

February 14, 2006

(Wördos? Friends who like to meet and talk about words. Anyone can do it! Wördos guiding principle: Do not talk about personal health or grandchildren at our meetings. If you do, you will be clobbered. ST = Mpls Star Tribune, PP = St. Paul Pioneer-Press, NYT = New York Times, unatt = don't know source, undtd = don't know date, re = regarding, head = headline, AHD = American Heritage Dictionary III, YFIO = you figure it out. Italics used freely for emphasis. All entries contributed by Wördos, all dates 2005's unless flagged.)

Our annual quiz: Forty-five persons, most of them young journalism students or news-writers, took the Wördos's annual grammar-spelling test two weeks ago at the MNA convention. There was good news, there was bad news. Most (33 of the 45) knew where to put apostrophes to form possessives. Most (34) knew to use *that* in a dependent clause, most (38) knew the difference between *appraise* and *apprise*. It was surprising though, that 23 (a bit more than half) believed that *alright* was all right, and that 18 believed it was correct to write "The dog *laid* on the chair." Twenty-five of the 45 didn't know what a *plurality* was (the most votes received, but fewer than half), and 24 flubbed *compared* with to *compared to*. The test was prepared by Wordo Fred Webber. – Ed.

Best of the worst, from our friends in TV:

"You can see the smoke *swarming over the city.*"
(Cindy Brucato, CH5, 12-27-'05)
"The fog will be few *and far between.*" (Unknown
weather-person, CH11, 11-25-'05)
"Hard and *steadfast* rules..." (CH11, 11-5-'05)
"We lacked *hardly any sunshine.*" (Weather-person, CH5, 1-5)
"I want to warn you to *be on your p's and q's.*" (C-span, 11-23)
"A few rumors have *went* around." (CNN, 1-17)

Agreement, lack of: "A graduate will earn $200,000 more in *their* (his, or recast) lifetime." TV commercial, unatt. 12-27-'05) "A group of soldiers *leave* (leaves) today." (CH5, 1-8) "Each *were* (was) given a pin." (CH5, 1-8 again). "(Actors will wear) the *ubiquitous* strips over their *nose* (noses) at play and rest ..." (ST, 1-1. *Ubiquitous*: Being everywhere at the same time. [AHD])" "(Car makers) are happy to sell cars to whomever wants *one* (them)." (PP, 12-28-'05)

Ambiguous references: "A surprising number of white-tailed deer *were seen driving* to our hunting sites..." (Wisconsin Outdoor News, 12-23-'05. Our italics!) "He served time for drug-related offenses at San Quentin ..." (ST, 1-8. This says the offenses for which he was imprisoned were committed while he was in prison.)

Conflate – the latest word dejour: It means join or bring together, but it has a trendy, with-it sound. "We need not *conflate* those singular attributes with the other side of the man." (Syl Jones, ST, 12-13-'05) "Reports *conflated* ... areas into one amorphous, afflicted 'third world.'" (San Diego Citybeat, 1-4) "Kennedy *conflated* the times report..." (NewsMax.com, Florida 1-1) "The war in Iraq was *conflated* with the war on terror." (Topeka Capital Journal, 12-29-'05) "He *conflated* (the) position with that of the school board..." (Ch. Sc. Monitor, 12-20-'05)

Huh? "Police are *investing* a robbery." (W.B.Press, 10-9-'05) "(He) *flaunted* (flouted) U.N. rules..." (ST, 12-4) A basketball player was identified as "Mugshot." (ST, 1-2. No first name.) On-screen instructions (CH5, 1-8): "Robb adlibs to anchor ... anchor adlibs back to Robb." Wördo Fred Webber received a phone message saying "We were just sitting around *comenserating*." "...his college teammate just happened to be *the most unique* of NFL entities." (Jim Souhan, ST, 1-4. Nope. *Unique*: one of a kind.) "Their marriage has survived 8 children (and spouses)." (ST, 12-29-'05. Eight of each?) "*Fictitious* town of Amityville..." (Jeff Passolt, KMSP-TV, undtd. No. It's a real town.) "(The Pope) *made due* ... with a skullcap." (PP, 12-23-'05) "(He uses his skills) to target immigrants and *convince* (persuade) them to sign documents." (PP-12-15-'05) "*Further* up the Mississippi ..." (ST, 12-18-'05. Wördo Peg Alnes: "No, dammit! *Farther*!") "... people say their *peace* (piece) and then it's forgotten." (PP, 12-29-'05) "Weaver ... *snucked* (sneaked) back." (PP-11-13-'05) "(The van) *grinded* (ground) against a median wall..." (PP, 12-29-'05) "TEEN FOUND DEAD" (CH11, 10-25-'05. He was 12 years old.) "(N.J. voted to) *disband* the death penalty." (NYT, 1-15. No. "Disband: To dissolve an organization – a corporation, for example." AHD) "Knight-Ridder would have to cut costs between $150 million to as much as $350 million. (Guild Reporter, 12-16-'05. Between $150 million and $350 million.) "*RIDING HERD* AGAINST MAD-COW" (ST, 11-20-'05, story about an attack on the disease. When cowboys rode herd they were controlling the herd, not attacking it.) "The Iron Range still *contain* (contains) the highest concentration of ore." (Rake, 12-'05) "(He) publishes a highly *irrelevant* (irreverent?) electronic newsletter." (Joe Nathan AOL column, 1-11)

Insinuate itself: "... electronic amplification has been *insinuating* itself into the opera house..." (ST, 2-8. It's a toss-up. AHD's first meaning of insinuate is "To introduce or otherwise convey ... gradually and insidiously." Its second meaning, though, might be a better fit for the ST quote. "To introduce by subtle or artful means." (Insinuate, to me, still carries the connotation of stealthiness, or harm. – Ed.)

Preposition problems: "BOSTON SCIENTIFIC CONFIDENT *ON* (of? about?) GUIDANT." (ST, 1-5) "... received a medal *in a* (for the) controversial fatal shooting of a teenager." (ST, 1-14)

Lie-lay: "Cast your stress aside, *lay* (LIE!) back and enjoy..." (ST, Lk.Minnetonka Style, Fall, '05) "She was *laying* (LYING!) in these leaves." (CH9, 10-26) "They want to *lay* (LIE!) back." (CBS, undtd) "(They) take time to *lay* (LIE!) down." (Chris Welch, ST, 10-3-'05)

Literature, critics: "The potter's literary debut is full of laughs and some decent advice, *debauching* conventional design wisdom and lobbing bon mots with abandon." (Kim Yeager, ST, 12-28-05. (Debauch: To corrupt morally." [AHD] Debunking, perhaps? Deploring?)

Preposition abuse: "I have never been as disappointed as I am *of* (in? with?) George Bush..." (Sen. Harry Reid ltr, 11-22-'05)) "It's difficult to understate the public interest *of* (in) returning war dead." (Quill, 9-'04. Did writer mean *overstate*?) "...between one store *to* (and) another." (CH5, 11-28-'05)

Typos, dangerous words: Newswriters learn, and learn painfully, that there are words which by themselves cause innocent and happy thoughts but that make great, big explosions when joined with certain other words. One explosive combination is *pen* followed by *is*, as in "the pen is mightier than the sword." This caused a celebrated typo in a headline (I believe it was in a Chicago daily newspaper. Can anyone attribute?) which should have read "GOVERNOR'S PEN IS BUSY OVER WEEKEND." An enterprising printer removed spaces between the words (deliberately?) which provided a somewhat different slant: "GOVERNOR'SPENISBUSYOVERWEEKEND." The same unfortunate combination, again caused by misplaced spacing material, was reported by a person at the recent M.N.A. convention in another headline: "THOMPSON'S PENIS A SWORD" Al Zdon, formerly Hibbing Daily Tribune editor, has another: "We ran a photo of a woman fleeing a burning village. Great anguish and distress on her face. The caption read: "Woman's but destroyed in fire" (Should have been hut, of course.)

TV: "The snow melted on the relatively mild ground." (Paul Douglas, CH4, 11-16-'05) "Any way this process could have been *shrunken*? (Fred Graman, Court TV, 11-'05) "This begs *for* the question." (KSTP-AM, 12-5-'05. Wordo Fred Webber: "No. Begging the question is what one does in an argument when one assumes what one claims to be proving. And you don't beg for the question.") "Let the chips fly where they fall," and "The tenements of socialism." (Both, Callers, KSTP-AM, 12-9-'05) "Move out of the Tice area..." (Mike Max, CH4, 1-2. Era?)

Who, for animals? No. Who is reserved for persons. "She rescued the poodle, *who* cannot walk..." (ST, 1-5. Wördo Webber, again: "A poodle ain't a who.")

— yr humble & obt svt, Robert MacGregor Shaw.

PREFACE

What this is not

Not to get off on a negative note, but this is not meant to be a thorough, comprehensive grammar guide. Far from it. There are many of those on the market. Maybe a thousand or more, all better and more complete than anything I could write. If you want one of those, I will recommend some.

What I hope this is

This is intended to be a follow-up to what Jeremiah Reedy wrote about the origins and derivations of words, how they were used originally, and weird words. I'm going to write about a more practical matter: the many words that are used or misused today. Some are used quite differently from not just their original meanings, but also fairly recent meanings.

This is simply a collection of the words and their uses that I've encountered over my relatively brief career proofreading. I haven't run into every word and every use. Just some fun and interesting ones. A lot of the examples come from contributions at Wördos grammar group meetings over the last twenty-plus years.

For whom is this part written?

This is not written for professional proofreaders, not even for unprofessional proofreaders. There are much better sources for both groups, notably books by Mary Norris (*Between You and Me: Confessions of a Comma Queen*) and Benjamin Dreyer (*Dreyer's English*).

My part of this philological adventure is to give examples of how the American English language is used today, principally in newspaper and broadcast journalism.

My interest started when I was very young and, moving forward, my education (B.A.in Journalism), 20-plus years as a member of the Wördos grammar group and 15-plus years of proofreading for Minnesota Outdoor News.

This won't be an exhaustive study of all that's wrong with grammar, usage, style, etc., just stuff (one of my favorite words, as you will see) some people might find interesting. I hope it will be more enjoyable than illuminating. (An Associated Press story about a fast-food place called it a burger joint. "Its vegetarian patties are available in some burger joints like Carl's Jr." AP Strib 5-3-19. So I can call stuff stuff.)

I'm not going to try to teach you anything. My hope is you'll find this interesting and sometimes provocative and fun to read.

I'm citing what I and fellow Wördos members consider the most frequent errors in newspapers, magazines, online, and in broadcasting. My objective is not to cover every conceivable type of error or malfunctioning punctuation mark. For example, I'll write about hyphens, but not en or em dashes. I'll write about commas, but not semicolons, or colons, for that matter. A very touchy matter lately. And I won't write about sentence fragments because I like to use them. Faster that way.

Sometimes books on grammar get so esoteric or pedantic that they don't apply to everyday life, e.g., when is the last time you bumped into parallel construction or the subjunctive mood in a way that was important to you?

Finally, remember, I'm a proofreader, not a writer. I don't mean to lower your expectations more than I already have, but this won't be a work from Fitzgerald or Hemingway.

George Orwell, though, has an interesting take that has the two activities seeming to overlap:

> [M]odern writing at its worst does not consist in picking out words for the sake of their meaning and inventing images in order to make the meaning clearer. It consists in gumming together long strips of words [that] have already been set in order by someone else, and making the results presentable by sheer humbug.

ACKNOWLEDGMENT

Most of the quotations in boxes appeared in Bryan Garner's "Usage Tip of the Day" email.

"Bryan Andrew Garner is an American lawyer, lexicographer, and teacher who has written more than two dozen books about English usage and style as well as advocacy. He also wrote two books with Justice Antonin Scalia: *Making Your Case: The Art of Persuading Judges* and *Reading Law: The Interpretation of Legal Texts*." (Wikipedia)

Other contributions from Bryan Garner are cited throughout the following pages.

CHAPTER V
Fred's Tale

How I got into this mess—the book

As mentioned, Professor Emeritus Jeremiah Reedy, Ph.D., hereafter referred to as Jeremiah, and I belong to Wördos. Jeremiah has already explained the history of Wördos and the reason for the umlaut. Unlike my learned, well-educated colleague and friend, I do not have an advanced degree. I barely earned—stretching the meaning of the word to an almost unbelievable extent—one.

About a year ago, maybe more, Jeremiah said he was going to write a book about etymology and asked if I'd be interested in contributing a part on proofreading. (Fortunately, I knew he wasn't talking about insects.)

I said no, I was too busy, and there already were more than a thousand books about words on the market. No one had expressed a need for a thousand one.

Besides, I was very reluctant to write a book about a subject that everyone was an authority on: grammar. Virtually everyone knew all the rules of grammar. *I* before *e* except after *c*. Don't start a sentence with *and* or *but*. Never use a double negative.

Whatever they learned in grade school were the rules of the grammar gods and were everlasting and immutable.

Eventually, however, I agreed. But in time, this "part" of the book reached co-author status, something I'd hoped to avoid. I'm a proofreader, not a writer. Writers write. Proofreaders proofread.

Jeremiah's purpose is to tell you about the origin of words and how things grammatical ought to be. Mine is to tell you how they are.

Amble, not preamble

I've always been interested in words and how they are used, especially how they are used effectively. In the mid-1960s, I was in a Psychological Warfare (now Operations) Company in the U.S. Army Reserve. That group, too, was interested in the effective use of words.

But long before that, I was curious.

I was born in Northeast ("Nordeast," as those who currently or at one time lived there) Minneapolis and spent the first 10 years of my life there. It was there that I discovered my interest in words.

As a child, I listened to the babushka-wearing ladies standing on the street corners talking. I didn't understand what they were saying. I thought that it was "adult language" that I would learn as I grew up. But it was Polish, and I never did learn it. However, it started my interest in language.

Throughout my challenging school years, the only subject I really paid attention to was English. In other courses, I caught up on lost sleep from the night before. In my senior year in high school and freshman year in college, I was exempt from taking English classes. My scores on the English parts of standardized tests were high enough to boost my overall scores to an impressive level.

I graduated with a B.A. (major Journalism, minor Humanities) from the University of Minnesota.

Most of my adult life was spent working for local advertising agencies in what was called account management. Athough it involved writing plans and proposals, it was not a position for writers. At one agency job, though, I worked with a couple of creative people who allowed me to make contributions to the creative effort. To everyone's surprise, I won some awards for writing.

Before Wördos there was nothing.

Sure, there were writers' groups. Maybe some grammar groups somewhere, but I never heard of them.

While working at Sable Advertising Systems in the 1990s, we received a letter with one of the ads we had produced for Polaris Industries. Someone had marked a couple of errors in the body copy of the ad. At first we were a bit irritated that some little old nitpicker had nothing better to do than to correct grammar and usage. But then, I became intrigued with the group, Wördos, that had sent the letter. I tracked down Peter Baxter, whose name was on the return address and asked about the group. He explained what the group did—catch mistakes in the media and notify the miscreants in hopes that they would correct the error of their ways, or at least their writing.

Peter invited me to the group's next meeting and I thanked him. However, I didn't intend to go because I felt that even though I had demonstrated some knowledge of grammar and usage, I'd be no match for professionals and they'd laugh at whatever I brought to the meeting. So, for a couple of years I didn't give it much thought.

I don't remember what happened to make me think about the group again, but I finally decided to attend a meeting to see exactly what they were up to.

It was a hoot!

The group talked about errors they had caught, argued about what certain words meant and how they were used, and, in general, just had a really good time.

My kind of people.

They weren't, as I thought they would be, pedantic, stuffy, lost in the past. They were people who enjoyed talking about the careful use of language and writing. Their key word, before there were key words, was clarity.

"You know what I mean."

"No, I don't know what you mean. I only know what you said or wrote."

Clarity

> *I just stop trying to sound important. I just say it. The simpler you say it, the more eloquent it is.*—August Wilson

American Heritage Dictionary, 4th edition (online): "*Clarity*—the quality of being coherent and intelligible."

As you read in Jeremiah's History of the Wördos, "We believe that the failure to write clearly jeopardizes understanding and believability, and that writing well is important in establishing credibility and competence."

Why words are important

In addition to their role in communicating with clarity, words are important because we make assumptions about others based on their language skills—how well they write and speak.

> *The existence of different manners of speech for persons in various ranks is a familiar fact. We are constantly sorting and classifying people according to them. A variation of any national language according to social levels is called class dialect. . . . When we talk, then, we tell much more about ourselves than the factual statements we are making. The sum total of small nuances will indicate much about our training, environment, economic position, and even profession. In conversation we are unconsciously providing a rich commentary about ourselves which supplements the clothing and outward possessions we gather.*—Margaret Schlauch

On a grander scale.

> *All the major achievements of humanity, and especially the accumulation and passing down of knowledge, rely on language.*—**Morton M. Hunt**

What is more powerful than a word? After all, what are thoughts without words? How could you think? How could you talk to yourself?

> *A tiny little word can be a clap of thunder.*—**French proverb**

Words make you happy

Words make you sad.
Words make you angry.
Words excite.
Words calm.
Words express love.
Words express hate.
Words shock.
Words teach.
Words hurt.
Words paint pictures.
Words bring back memories.

As Mark Twain said:

"The difference between the right word and the almost right word is the difference between lightning and a lightning bug.

"To get the right word in the right place is a rare achievement. To condense the diffused light of a page of thought into the luminous flash of a single sentence, is worthy to rank as a prize composition just by itself … Anybody can have ideas—the difficulty is to express them without squandering a quire of paper on an idea that ought to be reduced to one glittering paragraph.

"I notice that you use plain, simple language, short words and brief sentences. That is the way to write English—it is the modern way and the best way. Stick to it; don't let fluff and flowers and verbosity creep in. When you catch an adjective, kill it. No, I don't mean utterly, but kill most of them—then the rest will be valuable. They weaken when they are close together. They give strength when they are wide apart. An adjective habit, or a wordy, diffuse, flowery habit, once fastened upon a person, is as hard to get rid of as any other vice.

"Writing is easy. All you have to do is cross out the wrong words."

Sources and citations

> *The system used for citing references should be designed to give minimum interruption to readers' progress through the text. It should allow them to concentrate on primary information.*—**Christopher Turk & John Kirkman**

As I get into citing examples of the good, the bad, and the ugly in grammar and usage, I should release the secret code for understanding my sources and references. Please understand that I will not use any system that resembles what you may have learned about for citing references—bibliographies, footnotes, and Latin expressions, although I may cheat occasionally by using *ibid.*

My primary source for style is the *Associated Press Stylebook 2019* and, in some cases, *The Chicago Manual of Style.*

Rather than put the code in the back of the book, I'll put it here so you can recognize the sources as you read.

Abbreviations for Sources

AHD = *American Heritage Dictionary Online* Version 2.2.2

AP = *AP Stylebook* (online 2019)

GMAU = *Garner's Modern American Usage* (online)

NYT = *New York Times* (online)

ON = *Outdoor News**

PP = (St. Paul) *Pioneer Press* (online print)

Strib = (Minneapolis) *Star Tribune* (online and print)

WaPo = *Washington Post* (online)

WSJ = *The Wall Street Journal* (online and print)

Unk = Unknown**

*I often won't be able to cite a specific date for ON entries. When I first started collecting ON errors, I didn't expect to write a book so I didn't keep track of dates.

** Pretty much the same as above. This designation will appear for examples other than ON that I jotted down but failed to source because I never expected to have to cite them.

Where I have a source, I will show it. Usually, though, many of the examples I give are common words, uses or constructions. Strange as some might be.

Trust me, I didn't make them up.

Examples of unclear writing

I'm going to lump examples of dangling participles, ambiguous references, strange constructions, vagueness and mysteriousness together under this one heading. In some cases the distinctions are subtle and meaningless.

"Mental decline inevitable, but can be upgraded."
Strib 12-3-18 headline
[That's good?]

"… was held for the 30th time this year." ON
[30 times in one year, or this year for the 30th time?]

Friday I did my show with Jordanna Green from our cabin on Pelican Lake." Paul Douglas WCCO Radio 8-13-18
[They aren't married, not even going together. I doubt it was *our* cabin.]

"Student, adopted himself, raises money for adoptions" Strib headline 5-11-19

"A friend of King's." WaPo 4-6-19
[A friend of King's what?]

"I've got the best smile I could ever ask for in one day." Clear Choice Dental implant TV commercial
{He will have that smile for only one day.]

"You should browse the bags armed with some information." Article about shopping for dog food.
[Do armed dogs have anything to do with the Second Amendment? How can bags be armed with information?]

"Hillary Clinton warns of 'a full-fledged crisis in our democracy' at Yale." WaPo online 5-22-18
[Stay away from Yale; there will be a crisis there.]

"The incident occurred at a summit on water contamination at the EPA's headquarters in Washington." WaPo 5-23-18
[You'd think they'd be more careful at EPA headquarters.]

"I remember meeting a mother of a child who was abducted by the North Koreans right here in the Oval Office." George W. Bush, Washington, D.C., June 26, 2008
[The White House needs better security.]

From *Outdoor News*, dates unknown

For the last 15 years, I have been a part-time proofreader at Minnesota Outdoor News (ON). Later I'll explain how I was lucky enough to end up there. For now, though, I want to thank them for allowing me to use these examples. It's important to point out that they are taken before publication, i.e., they were caught in the proofreading process and did not appear in the final issue. It's important, too, to note that our columnists are freelance writers who are primarily outdoor enthusiasts. Their primary vocation/occupation is hunting and fishing, not writing.

I will cite examples from ON, but I won't name the writers! Biting the hand, so to speak. And most of the time, I can't supply dates because I started collecting many of the ON quotes long before I knew they might be needed for attribution in a book.

> "The Campaign to Save the Boundary Waters on March 5 announced that former ..."
> [Sounds like they're going to save the Boundary Water on only March 5]

> "Earlier this year, I was invited to hunt private land during the coffee hour at a country church I was attending."
> [Doesn't give you much time to hunt.]

> "A box turtle laid its eggs at his in-laws' last spring, and Brandon Kitts was on hand in September when they hatched."
> [His in-laws hatched?]

> "Up ahead, a boat tried unsuccessfully to anchor in the wind. Drawing nearer, I soon realized it as a buddy of mine."
> [It's good to have boats as buddies.]

> "A four-wheel drive pickup entered the fields and didn't close the gate. The cattle did considerable damage to the corn and other crops. They also drove in the wetland and got stuck."
> [The cattle got stuck? The pickup got stuck?]

> "Two southeast Iowa men pleaded guilty to illegal possession and trapping of turtles after they were cited by conservation officers ..."
> [The turtles were cited?]

"A 34-year-old Piedmont man has been charged with shooting a mountain lion without a license …"
[Where do mountain lions go to get licenses?]

"If you're planning to hunt in North Dakota this fall and think you might run into a turkey you can purchase one online."
[You can purchase a turkey online?]

"The daughter of a trapper, Tas grew up hunting, fishing and trapping with her father as their main source of food."
[Wonder how one prepares father for a meal?]

"Jason Mork … harvested these 13- and 8-point bucks that were locked together while party hunting in Lac qui Parle County."
[That will teach deer to party hunt.]

"When I walked into the doors of the Mayo Clinic …"
[Did it hurt?]

"Stinson, who is president of FHNB and is legally blind, said he has never seen another chapter …"
[I see.]

"So how do you prepare wild game like Scherwinski?"
[Scherwinski is a chef, not wild game. One might want to prepare wild game the way Scherwinski prepares it.]

"Matt, Wilfred, Clarence, Al and Paul Leyendecker … harvested these whitetails in 1946 from the land near Laport they've hunted for over a century."
[They must be very old hunters.]

"In a few short weeks …"
[Are some shorter than others?]

In most of the above examples, it's simply a matter of moving some words around to correct the statement. In others, the sentence may have to be rewritten. In all cases, the writer should read what was written to see if it makes sense.

Remember, there is nothing wrong with simple declarative sentences.

Some of the worst things ever written have been due to an avoidance of the ordinary word, and the mistaken choice of what the writer thought was a more dignified word or phrase.—**Henry Bett (1932)**

And, finally, these entries may not precisely fit this category, but I don't know where else to put them and they deserve some kind of recognition. You've probably seen these odd constructions almost every day in the obituaries, if you're at that stage in life where you read the obits. All of these are from the Strib.

He married his wife ...
She met her husband of 47 years ...
She is survived by her husband of 45 years and her lover.
She married her former husband.

And my all-time favorite (so far):

Tom and his deceased wife Jane ... then built an extremely successful (business). After Jane passed, Tom married his wife Alice. [Names changed to protect the innocent.]

CHAPTER VI
The Joys of Proofreading

The mess I'm in now

Let me be perfectly clear. The principal joy for me of proofreading is correcting others' writing. It's always fun to correct someone. Nothing can make you look smarter.

Judging by the errors in writing today—not just the abominable writing in texts and social media—but the numerous errors in even in the once-trusted so-called mainstream media: local newspapers and radio and TV stations, national newspapers, television networks and cable channels, and magazines—there's a lot of joy out there.

In the day, there were people called editors or copyeditors who were responsible for catching errors and correcting copy. As media (plural) have come under pressure to be more profitable, or just profitable, these positions have been eliminated. Cutting may save money, but it sure hasn't saved credibility. Most of us judge the credibility of a medium (singular), by how error-free it is. Not just a matter of truth, but a matter of accuracy in information and its presentation.

Are we going to hell in a handbasket? Is proofreading a lost art? Let's see.

Is Proofreading a Lost Art?

The New York Times Saturday Review of Books: Has the press grown so wayward in this era of rush and linotypes that its errors defy correction? Has exact proofreading in consequence become a lost art? Or, if not, why is it that the eyes of the careful reader must be so constantly offended by typographical inaccuracies?

I have just read Hilaire Belloc's "Robespierre," published by a leading New York house. The picturesque style of the author is marred by obscurities and strainings for effect. These, however, would offer little difficulty to the reader were they not frequently made twice as bad by the absence of intelligent punctuation – commas, semicolons, and dashes appearing sometimes to be inserted (or omitted) at haphazard.

True, no two authorities ever quite agreed on how to punctuate, and this, as well as the erratic style of capitalization, might be overlooked. But no one can justify the wedding of verbs and nouns whose differing numbers loudly forbid the banns, or other such elementary blunders in syntax. These may be due primarily to carelessness on the author's part, but surely they could have been rectified.

Still more annoying are some other errors. The Constituent Assembly is repeatedly referred to as the "Constituant," though sometimes the French femine, "Constituante," is used; the flight to Varennes becomes the "flight to Vincennes." The Hotel Britannique the "Hotel Brittannique," and Talleyrand "Tallyrand"; "Champs de Mars" is counterbalanced by "Rue des Petits Champ," Lebas is alternately "Le Bas," Robespierre's brother is now Augustin and now "Augustine," and the infamous editor of Pere Duchesne figures so nearly uniformly as "Herbert" that I should think that form had been adopted advisedly did the usual spelling. "Hebert," once or twice creep in to upset the supposition.

And worse remains to be told. What I have set down so far offended only my perhaps overcritical eye; but when I came full tilt on "valley forge" in all the ignominy of lower-case initials my patriotic gorge was roused, and I vowed by the shade of Washington to—register a protest.

F.C.W. MAY 3, 1902
The New York Times Archives

I hope you noted the date. Nothing new today.

Is proofreading an art? Once there was a difference between proofreading and copyediting. Proofreading was generally considered catching and correcting typos (since type is no longer set by mechanical means, a typo today is an operator error), spelling and punctuation. Copyediting was those activities plus making suggestions for rewriting for consistency and accuracy. Sometimes, though, just changing a word can change the meaning of a sentence or paragraph. If proofreading changes style and usage, is it still just proofreading?

And anyway, who needs proofreaders? Maybe these publications. (Errors are in boldface.)

Headline: Freshman-fueled Duke crushes **No. 2** Kentucky
Article: ... to lead Duke to an easy 118-84 victory over **No. 4** Kentucky ... Strib 11-7-18

"... so I **I** figured I'd have a party." Strib 7-9-19
"... with neighbors who prefer wildlife at **[a]** distance."... Strib 6-29-19
"... before throwing him down the stairwell where he was beaten again **[with]** wood from the banisters." Time online 7-19-19
"Two government officials aid **[said]**." WaPo 7-1-19

"Ocasio-Cortez's criticism came after a video fo [**of**] Ivanka Trump went viral over the weekend." Unk

"But he told me [**he**] never writes anything negative." C.J 6-29-19

"White couple gets pummeled on **on** freeway ..." Alternet 6-10-19

And my all-time favorite, from a 1963 issue of the *Star Tribune*: The Vikings drafted Northwestern's great [p]ass grabbing end Paul Flatley.

Before I launch into an almost never-ending list of more errors, not just typos, in today's media, let's agree to a really important point.

Things Change

Words sometimes change their proper historical meaning, and when the change is sanctioned by a general and established usage it must be accepted. On the other hand, we ought to resist any perversion of the meaning of the word as long as we can.—**Henry Bett**

Two things to keep in mind when discussing changes in language:

Prescriptive and descriptive grammar.
It's very much a matter of style.

Descriptive vs. Prescriptive

"There can be no 'correctness' apart from usage."—**Charles Carpenter Fries**

The above quote drives prescriptive grammarians crazy. So does this one:

> *Purism, whether in grammar or in vocabulary, almost always means ignorance. Language was made before grammar.*—**Thomas Hardy**

Prescriptive grammar means a person uses language as he or she thinks it ought to be used. It's like a doctor's prescription: it tells you how to use the medicine. Many former and some current teachers believe prescriptive is the best way to teach language, the "correct way."

Linguistics takes the prescriptive approach to language.

Descriptive grammar means a person uses language as it is spoken or written. For example, you've probably often heard someone admonish someone else not to use a double negative. However, what's wrong with, "Not unlike Trump standing by his assertion that four liberal/progressive Democratic congresswomen …" Alternet/Huffington Post 7-19-19

I hear or read a construction like that quite often, even by "better" speakers and writers.

A matter of style

In addition to descriptive and prescriptive grammar, syntax, usage, and spelling are very much a matter of style, not hard and fast rules. Every major medium, and even some minor ones, has* its own style manual. *The Associated Press Stylebook, The Chicago Manual of Style, The New York Times, The New Yorker* magazine—these and many others have their own styles and sometimes don't agree with each other. When they don't, it's not a matter of right or wrong, it's a matter of style.

*I'm still an old-fashioned guy. I often use *medium* as singular and *media* as plural.

In answering a rather long question to one of its editors regarding a disagreement about usage, the AP Stylebook replied, "Most if not all of these are matters of preference and sense of style, not actual grammar, and could go either way."

As an example of how different publications have different styles, here's how various publications treat the name of *The New Yorker* magazine.

> The Columbia Journalism Review (3-5-19 online) said, "published yesterday in *The New Yorker* ..." (Includes *The* [cap *T*) with *New Yorker.*)

> *The Wall Street Journal* (4-4-19) printed, "Condé Nast has tapped veteran media executive Roger Lynch as its new global chief executive as the publisher of ... and the (lower case *t*) New Yorker combines its U.S. and U.K. businesses."

> *The Washington Post* 3-5-19 (online) avoids the problems by avoiding the word *the*! "... thesis of New Yorker staff writer Jane Mayer's ..."

> But on 3-7-19, *The Washington Post* picked up *the* in "citing the New Yorker report on the network's close ties to Trump." Demonstrating there is no need for consistency if you're big enough.

> *The* (with a capital *T*) *New Yorker* has some stylistic differences of its own. Unlike the AP and many publications, it continues to capitalize the *p* in *president* after first reference to a U.S. president.

> ... Presidents Clinton and Bush

> former Presidents who were ...

> [Dates unknown.]

AP says, capitalize *president* only as a formal title before one or more names: *President Donald Trump, former Presidents Gerald R. Ford and Jimmy Carter.*

Lowercase in all other uses: *The president said Monday he will look into the matter. He is running for president. Lincoln was president during the Civil War.*

The New Yorker shows *Web site* as two words with a cap *W*, where almost all other publications and AP show one word *website*.

The New Yorker also puts a comma between the month and year, e.g., *December, 2014.*

The New Yorker often spells out numbers above 10 that other publications don't:

… a hundred (not *one* before *hundred*) and eighty-two women, seventeen of them pregnant (3-30-15)

Mary Norris, who wrote the outstanding book *Between You & Me: Confessions of a Comma Queen,* said about copy-editing at *The New Yorker*:

House style at The New Yorker follows a system of "close" punctuation. That means we like commas and use them to underscore meaning and syntax. Opening this week's issue (May 16, 2016) at random, I find a sentence that begins, "Igor Spetic, in Cleveland, suffered …" Those commas around "in Cleveland" indicate that there is only one Igor Spetic and he is in Cleveland. Without commas around "in Cleveland," the implication would be that this is the Cleveland Igor Spetic, as opposed to some other Igor Spetic, the one in, say, Boston. (Autocorrect is driving me crazy here with its insistence on spelling Spetic as Septic.) …

We also spell out numbers: three hundred thousand instead of 300,000. Why? Why not? The style editors of earlier generations made these decisions, and although we do change style from time to time ("interne" became "intern," "de-luxe" became "deluxe"), we are mostly content to leave it alone. We still hyphenate "teen-ager." We make "over all" two words as an adverb. (From Quora)

Someone once said, I don't think it was I, "Let's take the easy one first: Style manuals *advise*; they don't dictate. You're not obligated to follow any one style manual to the letter, unless the boss says so."

Examples of individual style from other publications

WaPo (3-17-19) says, "Okay," but AP says that's not OK: "Do not use okay."

Time magazine (3-7-19): "Members of the Richfield and Academy of Holy Angels Trap Team pose for a portrait before competing at the annual trap shooting championship in Alexandria, Minnesota on June 13, 2018."

AP says, "Place one comma between the city and the state name, and another comma after the state name, unless ending a sentence or indicating a dateline …"

NYT uses Mr. and Mrs. Titles when referring to people in subsequent references.

And here, just because it's fun to read, are Wolcott Gibbs' rules for proofreading *The New Yorker* … in 1937.

In 1937, Wolcott Gibbs, an editor at The New Yorker magazine, wrote the "Theory and Practice of Editing New Yorker Articles." Although written in a "light spirit," (Gibbs was also a noted humorist) it was a working document at the magazine. Here are some examples of his guidance.

THEORY AND PRACTICE OF EDITING
NEW YORKER ARTICLES

THE AVERAGE CONTRIBUTOR TO THIS MAGAZINE IS SEMI-LITERATE; that is, he is ornate to no purpose, full of senseless and elegant variations, and can be relied on to use three sentences where a word would do. It is impossible to lay down any exact and complete formula for bringing order out of this underbrush, but there are a few general rules. [I selected a few of the original 31 rules.]

- Writers always use too damn many adverbs. On one page, recently, I found eleven modifying the verb "said": "He said morosely, violently, eloquently," and so on. Editorial theory should probably be that a writer who can't make his context indicate the way his character is talking ought to be in another line of work. Anyway, it is impossible for a character to go through all these emotional states one after the other. Lon Chaney might be able to do it, but he is dead.

- Our employer, Mr. Ross, has a prejudice against having too many sentences begin with "and" or "but." He claims that they are conjunctions and should not be used purely for literary effect. Or at least only very judiciously.

- See our Mr. Weekes on the use of such words as "little," "vague," "confused," "faintly," "all mixed up," etc., etc. The point is that the average *New Yorker* writer, unfortunately influenced by Mr. Thurber, has come to believe that the ideal *New Yorker* piece is about a vague, little man helplessly confused by a menacing and complicated civilization. Whenever this note is not the whole point of the piece (and it far too often is) it should be regarded with suspicion.

- This magazine is on the whole liberal about expletives. The only test I know of is whether or not they are really essential to the author's effect. "Son of a bitch," "bastard" and many others can be used whenever it is the editor's judgment that

that is the only possible remark under the circumstances. When they are gratuitous, when the writer is just trying to sound tough to no especial purpose, they come out.

- Mr. Weekes said the other night, in a moment of desperation, that he didn't believe he could stand any more triple adjectives. "A tall, florid and overbearing man called Jaeckel." Sometimes they're necessary, but when every noun has three adjectives connected with it, Mr. Weekes suffers and quite rightly.
- The more "as a matter of facts," "howevers," "for instances," etc., you can cut out, the nearer you are to the Kingdom of Heaven.
- Writers also have an affection for the tricky or vaguely cosmic last line.
- On the whole, we are hostile to puns.
- Try to preserve an author's style if he is an author and has a style. Try to make dialogue sound like talk, not writing.

Examples of changes over time

> *English usage is sometimes more than mere taste, judgment, and education—sometimes it's sheer luck, like getting across a street.*—**E.B. White**

And, as pointed out earlier, it's not just style, it's constant change in our language that's sometimes hard to keep up to.

Two words to one

One simple and visible example of change over time is the transition of two words to one, often using a hyphen as a transitional form.

I first noticed this trend while watching a 1930s movie. There was a theater marquee announcing an upcoming performance. It said the performance would take place "to-night." That made me wonder about other examples of "two to one words." Here are some examples:

Afterthought
Aftereffects
Bowhunter
Businesspeople
Creditworthiness
Decadeslong
Decisionmaking
Laughingstock
Postrecession
Postretirement
Schoolteachers
Timeframe
Undersecretary
Whitecollar

Changes in meanings of words

Over time, many words have changed from their original meanings, sometimes becoming the complete opposite of what they were intended to mean.

A frequently cited example is *awful*. In its original meaning in Old English, "awe" referred to "fear, terror or dread." It then took on a solemn or reverential sense of wonder, and "awful" and "awesome" meant the same as awe-inspiring. Then, "awful" took on a very negative connotation, and finally the word found its modern-day meaning of extremely bad. "Awesome," meanwhile, evolved in the opposite way, probably in the mid-1900s, and came to mean extremely good.

Redacted has been much in use lately. It once meant simply organized or edited. The word's use and meaning stretch back to ancient Rome and, later, Thomas Jefferson before it became a term for concealing sensitive text, as in the release of the Mueller report.

In the context of the Mueller report, *redacted* means "edited especially in order to obscure or remove sensitive information," Merriam-Webster says. Text is concealed to obscure several categories of subjects, color-coded in the document: grand jury testimony, classified information, ongoing investigative matters, and information that would, in Mr. Barr's words, "unduly infringe on the personal privacy and reputational interests" of peripheral players. Some of the redactions blot out entire pages. (Ben Zimmer WSJ.)

Other words that have changed meaning over time

From Culture Trip:

Cute

"A shortening of the word 'acute', 'cute' originally meant sharp or quick-witted, and was even written with an apostrophe in place of the missing A. In 1830s America, it took on a new significance and came to mean attractive, pretty or charming—though we still use it in its original manner in phrases like 'don't get cute with me', referring to someone trying to be clever."

Literally

"At one time literally was used only to refer to things that were actually happening – in the true and literal sense—'literally' is now used by many people for emphasis. It's a favourite of ex-footballer Jamie Redknapp, who came out with one-liners like 'these balls now—they literally explode off your feet' and 'he had to cut back inside onto his left, because he literally hasn't got a right foot.' Language pedants take note, though: this misuse is now so widespread the Oxford English Dictionary has altered its definition."

Myriad

"Nowadays, a myriad is an extremely large, uncountable number of things. Rewind to Ancient Greece, though, and a myriad specifically referred to the number 10,000. In Aegean numerals (used during the Bronze Age), it was represented by the symbol of a circle with four dashes."

From Mental Floss:

Egregious

"Egregious now describes something outstandingly bad or shocking, but it originally meant remarkably good. It comes from the Latin *ioceses*, meaning 'illustrious, select'—literally, 'standing out from the flock,' from *ex-*, 'out of,' and *greg-*, 'flock.' Apparently the current meaning arose from ironic use of the original."

Naughty

"In the 1300s, naughty people had naught (nothing); they were poor or needy. By the 1400s, the meaning shifted from having nothing to being worth nothing, being morally bad or wicked. It could refer to a licentious, promiscuous, or sexually provocative person, or someone guilty of other improper behavior. In *Sermons preached upon Several Occasions* (1678), Isaac Barrow speaks of 'a most vile, flagitious man, a sorry and naughty Governour as could be.' But in the same century, 'naughty' also had a gentler meaning, especially as applied to children: mischievous, disobedient, badly behaved."

Nice

"A few centuries ago if a gentleman called a lady 'nice,' she might not know whether to flutter her fan or slap his face. Nice entered English via Anglo-Norman from classical Latin *nescius*, meaning ignorant. Then it wandered off every which way. From the 1300s through 1600s it meant silly, foolish, or ignorant. During that same time period, though, it was used with these unrelated or even contradictory meanings:

•   Showy and ostentatious, or elegant and refined

- Particular in matters of reputation or conduct; or wanton, dissolute, lascivious
- Cowardly, unmanly, effeminate
- Slothful, lazy, sluggish
- Not obvious, difficult to decide, intricate

By the 1500s, 'nice' came to mean meticulous, attentive, sharp, making precise distinctions. By the 18th century, it acquired its current (and rather bland) meaning of agreeable and pleasant, but other meanings hung on, just to keep things interesting."

Changes in style

Other, more subtle but nevertheless important, changes have to do with changes in style.

Perhaps one of the most recent examples that many grammarians have trouble accepting is the use of the pronoun *they* with singular antecedents.

Everyone/his—For decades, everyone was considered singular and took a singular pronoun: Everyone brought his axe. About 15 years ago, the Wördos considered this the most frequent error in the media.

More recently, giving in to overwhelming wrong usage, and a hint of PC, the AP granted that it's OK to use everyone has *their* with *everyone.*

They, them, their—In most cases, a plural pronoun should agree in number with the antecedent: *The drivers like the cars they rented. They/them/I* are OK in some cases as a singular and or gender-neutral pronoun, if alternative wording is overly awkward. However, rewording usually is possible and preferable. AP

Regarding style and how flexible it is, the AP Stylebook online fielded the following question: "If I understand correctly, AP style prefers half-marathon to be hyphenated but ultramarathon to be one word. That seems inconsistent. Should ultra-marathon be hyphenated? Thanks for the guidance."

Their answer? "Indeed, it appears inconsistent; that's often the way of the language."

The old reliable Wikipedia says it best:

Singular they is the **use** in English of the **pronoun they** or its inflected or derivative forms, them, their, theirs, and themselves (or I), as an epicene (gender-neutral) **singular pronoun**. It typically occurs with an unspecified **antecedent**, as in sentences such as: "Somebody left their umbrella in the office.

Loan

Another example that is still exasperating to many grammarians— and Judge Judy—is the use of the word *loan* as a verb. They, and she, insist it's a noun.

However, AHD infuriates descriptive grammarians by allowing: **Loan**- verb [with obj.] borrow (a sum of money or item of property): *the word processor was loaned to us by the theater |he knew Rob would not loan him money.*

But, to prove our contention that it's a matter of style, *The New York Times Manual of Style and Usage* says don't you dare do it. "Do not use *loan* as a verb. Use *lend*, and in the past tense *lent* rather than *loaned*."

The Chicago Manual of style says, "The verb ***loan*** is standard especially when money is the subject of the transaction—but ... even then, **lend** appears somewhat more frequently in edited

English. ***Loan*** is the noun … corresponding to both ***lend*** and ***loan***, vb. The past-tense and past-participial form of lend is ***lent***…."

Go figure.

In 2015, the American Dialect Society voted *they* as the gender-neutral singular pronoun Word of the Year. The society recognized the pronoun's use in referring to a known person in order to avoid problems with the gender binary *he* or *she*.

During the "What's New in the 2019 AP Stylebook" session at the ACES (American Copy Editors Society) national conference in Providence, Rhode Island, a number of changes to the AP Stylebook were announced.

Here are some of the changes.

> Allowing accent marks in names, moving from the word percent when paired with an amount to the % symbol.

> A new entry that says the word "data" generally should take a singular verb and pronoun. So it is "the data is." [There are exceptions.]

> An entry in the section covers guidance not to use the terms "blacks" or "whites" as plurals. And the AP has dropped the hyphen from dual-heritage terms such as African American and Asian American.

> The section now says: "Consider carefully when deciding whether to identify people by race. Often, it is an irrelevant factor and drawing unnecessary attention to someone's race or ethnicity can be interpreted as bigotry."

That new entry, in part, says:

Racist, racism

Racism is a doctrine asserting racial differences in character, intelligence, etc., and the superiority of one race over another, or racial discrimination or feelings of hatred or bigotry toward people of another race.

The terms racism and racist can be used in broad references or in quotations to describe the hatred of a race, or assertion of the superiority of one race over others. The townspeople saw their votes as a rejection of racism.

No hyphen is needed if the modifier is commonly recognized as one phrase, such as "chocolate chip cookie" and "third grade teacher,"

The AP also no longer calls for hyphenations in double-e combinations like reelect, preempt and reenactment.

Perhaps the greatest influence on changes in meanings, spellings, style, and usage has been the internet.

According to *Time Magazine* (online 7-19-19), "Gretchen McCulloch's new book, *Because Internet: Understanding the New Rules of Language*, is a homage to ... linguistic metamorphosis—evolution made possible by the ascendance of the web and the unprecedented explosion of informal writing that has come with it. Her aim is to explain how the Internet has shaped language, as billions of people have become authors and found ways to type out the flirtations (☺) and frustrations (aklefj;awkjfdsafjka!!!) and quotidian blurghs that for centuries existed only as informal speech."

As one who rarely uses social media, texts, or tweets, I thank whatever gods may be that I'm being spared from this evolution.

Inclusiveness, called political correctness, has also played a role, albeit a lesser one, in changes to the English language. The Berkeley, California, City Council recently (July 2018) changed some of the language in its city code to be more gender neutral. For example, "manhole" will change to "maintenance hole."

Words that haven't changed but should

Taping a conversation—recording?
Shooting a film or *taping* a film—videoing (yes, seriously)
Dialing a phone—What's the alternative? Punching a phone? Pressing a letter or number?

Myths, common mistakes

The double negative

Perhaps no myth is more often quoted than, "Don't say that, it's a double negative." The corrector smiles smugly, believing he or she has just nailed a grammatical error that indicates the speaker or writer is from a part of the country where they don't know nothing.

It ain't necessarily so.

"There are no lengths she would not go to."
No less than Sherlock Holmes "Scandal in Bohemia" radio 1954

"Lucretius was not without his contradictions" WSJ 5/18-19-18

"… not unlike rewiring a nuclear submarine." Bill Farmer

"That thought was not incorrect." Strib 4-25-19.

"It's not an unusual sight." Unk

I haven't figured this one out yet

> "I humbly call on Minnesotans neither to needlessly condemn her nor to assume that we will not be seeing greater things from her."
> Letter to Editor, Strib 4-22-19

And/But

Another popular injunction, especially from those who learned or taught English in the 1950s, is to never start a sentence with *and* or *but*.

The Chicago Manual of Style says:

> There is a widespread belief—one with no historical or grammatical foundation—that it is an error to begin a sentence with a conjunction such as *and, but* or *so*. In fact, a substantial percentage (often as many as 10 percent) of the sentences in first-rate writing begin with conjunctions. It has been so for centuries, and even the most conservative grammarians have followed this practice.

> Both *Garner's Modern American Usage* and *Fowler's Modern English Usage* call this belief a superstition. *The Merriam-Webster Dictionary of English Usage* ... says, "Everybody agrees that it's all right to begin a sentence with *and*," and notes that you can find examples of it all the way back to Old English.

And then there's the rule of a thousand exceptions.

I before e except after c

How old is this rule? Some say it goes back, in another form, thousands of years:

It's eye before flea,
except after sea.

BIZARROCOMICS.COM

As Christopher Ingraham pointed out in WaPo (June 28, 2017):
Or, as an enterprising Redditor recently put it:

I before E...

...except in a zeitgeist of feisty counterfeit heifer protein freight heists reining in weird deified beige beings and their veiny and eidetic atheist foreign schlockmeister neighbors, either aweigh with feigned absenteeism, seized by heightened heirloom forfeitures (albeit deigned under a kaleidoscope ceiling weighted by seismic geisha keister sleighs) or leisurely reimbursing sovereign receipt or surveillance of eight veiled and neighing Rottweilers, herein referred to as their caffeinated sheik's Weimaraner poltergeist wieners from the Pleiades.

Ending a sentence with a preposition

Arguably, Winston Churchill said, "This is the sort of English up with which I will not put." Some sources say it's more likely he said, "This is the sort of bloody nonsense up with which I will not put," but there was concern about using the offensive word "bloody."

In all but the most formal writing, ending a sentence with a preposition is not a problem.

Splitting infinitives

Nobody says it better. From AHD:

Split infinitive (noun): a construction consisting of an infinitive with an adverb or other word inserted between *to* and the verb, e.g. *she seems to really like it.*

Usage
Is it wrong to use a **split infinitive**, separating the infinitive marker *to* from the verb? If so, then these statements are grammatically incorrect: *you have **to** really **watch** him*: ***to boldly***

go *where no one has gone before.* Writers who long ago insisted that English could be modeled on Latin created the "rule" that the English infinitive must not be split: *to clearly state* violates this rule; one must say *to state clearly.* But the Latin infinitive is one word (e.g., *amare,* 'to love') and cannot be split, so the rule is not firmly grounded, and treating two English words as one can lead to awkward, stilted sentences. In particular, the placing of an adverb in English is extremely important in giving the appropriate emphasis.

Got

Perfectly acceptable past participle of "get." Worse yet, for some people, "gotten" is acceptable, too.

None

None is the word that long ago alerted me to bad advice from former teachers of English. One, in particular, vehemently, almost violently, insisted that "none" is always singular because it's a contraction of "not one."

True, it usually means no single one and then takes singular verbs and pronouns; however, there are other uses, e.g., if the sense is no two or no amount of these things, e.g., "none of the teachers agree..." a plural verb can be used. "None of the bills have been paid."

Common errors

There are, of course, genuine errors that your teachers or mothers may have warned you about. Unfortunately, though, even these change.

A few years after I started attending Wördos meetings, I was invited to join the "10 Most Common Errors" Traveling Show. It was a SWAT (Special Wördos Attack Team) that visited newspapers throughout this great land (Minnesota) of ours, from Rochester to the Twin Cities. We met with the editorial staffs (news writers, not editorial writers) at papers such as the Rochester *Post Bulletin*, the *Twin Cities Pioneer Press*, the *Southwest Journal*, and the *Star Tribune*. Before I joined it, the grammar correction team (charged with seeking and destroying bad grammar, syntax, style, and usage) had also visited TV and radio stations.

We brought along the 10 Most Common Errors in the media as determined by researching our monthly newsletters over the previous fifteen years.

In addition to Phearless Phred, the team consisted of:

Marlene Reuber ...

has a master's degree in library science from Simmons College/Boston (undergrad degree from the University of Minnesota). She worked at libraries in Honolulu, Miami and St. Paul, and had a twenty-year career as Newsroom Administrator at Minnesota Public Radio. Her first "real" job: Fingerprint searcher in Washington, D.C. at the FBI. She says her fun jobs were editing a shopping guide in Lisbon, Portugal, and teaching modeling in San Francisco.

Bob Shaw ...

If we had a president or chairman, Bob would be the guy. He's the one who ran our meetings, spoke on our behalf, and initiated and moved projects along. Bob has two degrees, a B.A. in Philosophy and a Master's Degree in Journalism, both from the University of Minnesota. He worked for AP for several years and on *The Stars & Stripes* during WWII. He was manager of the Washington State Newspaper Publishers Association for a number of years before becoming manager of the Minnesota Newspaper Association for 17 years. He loves to travel, especially to Germany, and has written a number of books, including the award-winning *Bachelor Slob in the Kitchen*.

Jeremiah Witt ...

(Now deceased) Earned his undergraduate degree at the University of Wisconsin – Madison. He received his graduate degree at the University of Minnesota. He was a professor of chemistry for 37 years at Winona State University.

John "Jack" Finnegan …
(Now deceased)

Jack completed a B.A. in Journalism and Political Science at the University of Minnesota. Early in his career, he worked at the Post-Bulletin as a reporter. In 1951, he started as a night-side general assignment reporter for the then-*St. Paul Pioneer Press.* He became associate editor of the *Pioneer Press* editorial page, then executive editor. He retired in 1989 as senior vice president and assistant publisher.

What everyone had in common was a love of words and language.

One of the media we visited was Outdoor News Publications, publisher of six tabloid newspapers that cover Minnesota, Wisconsin, Ohio, Illinois, Pennsylvania, and New York. It is a rare successful print medium that has also entered the digital age.

After our presentation, the publisher asked me if I would be interested in joining the staff of the Minnesota edition as a proofreader. I admitted I knew nothing about fishing or hunting. He said that was OK, his columnists didn't know much about grammar, style, and usage. His news people did, but they didn't have time to proof most of the columnists.

I said, "you bet." That was almost 15 years ago, and it's been one of the enjoyable experiences of my life. Great people to work for.

But back to 2003. The Wördos had set out to determine the most common errors in media, believing a few errors probably represented 80% (newly AP-approved use of percentage sign!) of all errors. By identifying these errors we could help media reduce them and improve clarity of communication.

A properly constituted Wördos committee analyzed more than nine years of our monthly columns in the Minnesota Newspaper Association bulletin.

It's interesting, if not educational, to compare the most common errors then to (or is it with?) the most common errors today. Not much has changed. Here were the results:

10 Most Common Errors—Then

1. **Pronoun-Antecedent Lack of Agreement**
   "Everybody has *their* car here."

2. **Ambiguous Reference**
   "He wrote a $700 check for a pickup truck, *which later bounced*."

3. **Malapropisms**
   "The very *pineapple* of politeness."

4. **Preposition Problems**
   "... a vocal opponent *to* the Met Council"

5. **Lie/Lay Confusion**
   "Please *lay* down on the bed."

6. **Subject-Verb Lack of Agreement**
   "One in 10 *are* being hired."

7. **Fewer-Less Confusion**
   "*Less* than two goals a game."

8. **Vowel Changes in Past Tense**
   "Net assets *shrunk*."

9. **Verbification of Nouns**
   "He *offices* at home."

10. **Abuses of Unique**
   "... *very* unique performance."

Sadly, the Minnesota Newspaper Association no longer publishes a monthly Wördos column, so I'm no longer able to access a handy compendium of frequent errors. Therefore, I will list the most common errors I encounter while proofreading at *Minnesota Outdoor News*. Again, I appreciate the owners and managers allowing me to quote material from ON. And again, again, these errors were corrected **before** the writers' columns were published.

I would add the following to the list of **10 Most Common Errors—Then:**

More than 10 Most Common Errors—Now

Only—I admit to being obsessed with the misplacement of *only*. If nobody else seems to care, why should I? Because somebody has to! AHD joins in my concern:

> In normal, everyday English, the tendency is to place *only* as possible in the sentence, generally just before the verb, and the result is rarely ambiguous. Misunderstandings are possible, however, and grammarians have debated the matter for more than two hundred years. Advice varies, but in general, ambiguity is less likely if *only* is placed as close as is naturally possible to the word(s) to be modified or emphasized. *I saw her only once* stresses the single instance; *I only saw her once* leaves it unclear whether she was heard (or otherwise perceived) in addition to being seen.

Unless otherwise noted, these examples are from ON with no dates or attribution.

> "You might only keep these fish under you for 10 minutes."
> [You might keep these fish under you for only 10 minutes.]

> "You'll only have to pack those that you'll need that day."
> [You'll have to pack only those that you'll need that day.]

"We only saw whitetails." [We saw only whitetails.]

"Most of us only have a few days to hunt." [Most of us have only a few days to hunt.]

The placement of *only* may seem picky, and in some cases it's hard to see why it makes a difference. After all, you only live once, right?

Here's an example of the difference placement can make. I've picked a sentence from a TV commercial for a local company.

Bonfe Heating and Cooling: "We only hire the best."

As written, it could mean, "We don't torture them." "We don't listen to them." "We don't pay them."

There's and here's (Subject-verb disagreement)

"There's 10 steps to success." (Unk)

"Here's five ways to do that." (Unk)

"There's just 10 pages." (Unk)

"There's two things wrong with this premise." John Atcheson/ Common Dreams June 23, 2019

"And there's lots of people like Ronny Jackson, Andy Puzder, and Stephen Moore who never got the jobs Trump wanted to put them up for." WaPo online 6-24-19

And subject [what??] agreement

"The vast majority of hunters don't have these fine-tuned tricks up their sleeve[s]." ON

Continuously or continually

"Stillwater is *continuously* voted the best ..."
(Minnesota Mensa) Mensagenda July 2019

Continually should be used to mean very often or at regular or frequent intervals. *Continuously* should be used to mean unceasingly, constantly or without interruption. In the Mesagenda case, *continually* or *consistently* would have been better choices.

The reason is because

Not "because," use "is that" or just "is."

Two or more subjects treated as one

"Biden's centrism, his big mouth, his age and out-of-touchness, and his handsiness sets [set] him up ..." Salon's Amanda Marcotte tweeted. 6-17-19

"The snow depth and good ice now gives you complete silence." ON

"A little elbow grease and a few tools is all it takes." ON

As instead of because

As may be misunderstood as having its more usual meaning "while," during, since, etc., even at the beginning of a sentence. H.W. Fowler states: "To causal or explanatory *as*-clauses, if they are placed before the main sentence ... there is no objection." This is most common in British English—e.g.: "*As* she didn't get the original money, could she please have the larger sum?" Martin Waller, "Mail Shot," *Times* (London), 30 May 1997.

In many sentences, *as* is ambiguous, because it might be unclear whether it expresses time or cause.

> "As many Mensans love to talk, there will be discussions …" (Minnesota Mensa) Mensagenda July 2019

> Most common: "Please listen carefully as our menu has changed" as (!) used on many recorded messages.

> And the problem has been around for a long time. Listening to "The Lineup," a radio show from the early '50s, I heard: "Do not pay too much attention to their answers as they often lie."

> "… looking for the last hens of spring, as the majority have been bred." ON

> "Striking up a conversation then with a random bird is easier, as they're looking for you." ON

> "… especially with birds in sight, as you're trying to mimic a group of feeding hens…" [Close call, though. Could mean "while you're trying to mimic," which would be OK.)

> Finding good bait can be tough, as many bait shops have closed. ON

> Late-May crappies will smash an artificial just fine, as they are active and aggressive. ON

> "ABC did indeed cancel the series after a single season, as its ratings declined …" POP Culture Q&A Strib 6-17-19
> [Could mean either while or because!]

Unnecessary *of*

> "Too lenient of a deal." NBC News 7-10-19
> (Skip the *of.*)

Couple years

Add the *of.*
"… on a popular walleye river a couple [**of**] years ago."

As a noun, *couple* requires *of* between *couple* and *years*. Using *couple* as an adjective directly before the noun is unidiomatic and awkward.

When *couple* is used with comparison words such as *more, fewer,* and *too many,* the *of* is omitted, e.g., "Have a couple more shrimp." GMAU

Subject singular or plural?

"On this hallowed island there has been feast and famine …"

Some folks are fooled by the belief that the subject is always the first noun or pronoun in a sentence. As the above sentence demonstrates, that's not always the case. Take the time to think about it. This is very similar to the incorrect use, cited above, of *there's* and *here's.*

Different from/different than

… noticed Ziegler's run-up was different than what he saw
Souichi Terada Strib 7-14-19

Use from in almost all cases.

Farther/Further

Farther refers to physical distance. Further, everything else.

Examples? Virtually every TV weather forecaster in the country! Listen to them describe what will happen "further to the east" or "further south." And while I'm ranting about it (didn't use upper case, though), the same weather forecasters talk about *tempertures.* Probably the same folks who say, *con-tro-vers-ial* instead of *con-tro-ver-shull.*

If it were really important to me, and judging by the number of times I yell it at the TV set it should be, I'd write to every weather forecaster in the Twin Cities: "Ninety percent of the time you'll be right with farther. And 100% of the time you'll be right if you pronounce it tem-per-at-ture. Not tem-per-ture."

But the problem is bigger than the weather or the Twin Cities. Time Magazine (online 4-30-19) wrote, "Over the weekend, he went farther in a rally in Wisconsin, inaccurately claiming that children are actually put to death after birth."

"He ... was walking up further down the road." Strib 11-7-18

One

"Just 1 in 5 Minnesotans claim a church affiliation." Strib 9-23-19

In addition to the wrong verb, *1* and *5* should be spelled out.

"One in three people with necrotizing fasciitis die from the infection."
NBC News 6-30-19

"About one in five say the measures are about right." WaPo 6-17-19

Lie/Lay

How many times lately has a medical professional (nurse, technician, etc.) told me to lay on the table? Let me count them. I encountered one—out of hundreds—who asked me to *lie down.* I asked him how he knew that was correct. He said, as others have, that his mother taught him! In this case, mother was right.

Even Mensa (Mensa Bulletin March 2019) can't get it right: "… must have been standing against a wall or laying down …"

A lesson I have learned through the years: it's almost impossible to teach the rules for lie and lay. You have to develop an "ear" for it. But I'll give you one more chance.

The action word is *lay*. It takes a direct object. *Laid* is the form for its past tense and its past participle. Its present participle is *laying*.

Lie also has various other meanings, including to recline, to be situated or to exist. It does not take a direct object. Its past tense is *lay*. Its past participle is *lain*. Its present participle is *lying*.

When *lie* means to make an untrue statement, the verb forms are *lie, lied, lying*. (AP)

Why grammarians make poor poets.

I'm sorry to say
That if I had my way
At home I would stay
And in my bed I would lie

Anxious/Eager

To be anxious is to fear; to be eager is to look forward to. At least that's the way my mother explained it.

Impact

Used repeatedly (nine times in one ON column!). Try *affected, influenced, clobbered, bashed, hit* and just about any other verb that means the same thing.

Healthy/Healthful

Healthy = not sick. Healthful = conducive to health. Avoid "healthy fruits and vegetables."

Less/Fewer

Less—can't be counted. Fewer can be.

Myself/Me

Never substitute *myself* for *I* or *me*.

Unique

An absolute. Can't be modified, e.g., *very unique.*

Younger than her/Bigger than him and similar

"McConnell is up for reelection this cycle in Kentucky, where Trump is more popular than him ..." WaPo 11-15-18

I use a complete sentence, usually adding *is* or *are*, to see the obviously proper pronoun, e.g., "I am younger than she is."

Battles we've lost or are losing

Who/Whom

Who is the subject of a sentence. Whom refers to the object of a verb or preposition.

When in doubt, try this simple trick: If you can replace the word with *he* or *she*, use *who*. If you can replace it with *him* or *her*, use ***whom***.

Almost an honest mistake: KARE 11 5-26-19

"Police are looking for whomever shot her.: May look correct at first glance, but no, it's not. I sent a sentence similar to this one to AP's Ask the Editor.

Question from Medina, Minn. on June 16, 2016:

"I want to give it to whoever is in charge" or "I want to give it to whomever is in charge"? Thanks.

Answer

... to whoever is in charge. The grammatical guidance is to use who when it follows a preposition as the subject of the subsequent clause. The sentence should read as follows: I want to give it to whoever is in charge. (Or ... to the person in charge.)

Media/medium

Until a few years ago, I fought for this distinction: Media is plural, "There are many types of media in the country."; Medium is singular, "Radio is a medium." The AP backs me up on this one:

Generally takes a plural verb, especially when the reference is to individual outlets: *Media are lining up for and against the proposal.* The word is often preceded by "the." Sometimes used with a singular verb when referring to media as a monolithic group: *The media plays a major role in political campaigns.*

It's me

Traditionally, when a pronoun follows a linking verb, such as "is," the pronoun should be in the nominative case. So it's correct to say, "It is I." Not so surprisingly, many "modern" grammarians say "It is I" is pedantic. I don't care, I'm sticking with it because my learned friends expect it of me.

Older than her

Instead of ending with her, add is and you'll see "older than she is" works.

Bad/badly

Confusion in the use of **bad** versus **badly** usually has to do with verbs called copulas, such as *feel* or *seem*. Thus, standard usage calls for *I feel bad*, not *I feel badly*. As a precise speaker or writer would explain, *I feel badly* means "I do not have a good sense of touch." AHD

It's/its

Many people think *it's* is possessive because it seems to have a possessive letter *s*. Not so fast! The apostrophe *s* indicates a contraction, where something has been left out like *can't* and *don't*. Use an apostrophe when you mean it is or it has. *It's nice out.*

And to add to the confusion, when using its as a possessive, don't use an apostrophe. *The dog hurt its tail.*

Affect/Effect
Affect usually is a verb, and means to impact (sorry) or change.
Effect is usually a noun, and is the result of a change.

Neither–nor
'Doomsday Math Neither Accurate or [**nor**] Helpful' WSJ head
over letter to editor 7-8-19

"Neither Noor or [**nor**] his partner ..." WCCO-TV 4-15-19

This phrasing [neither/or] is either a serious grammatical lapse
or a serious typographical error. GMAU

Criteria/Criterion — Criteria = plural; Criterion = singular
But the criteria that ultimately triggered probationary status
was the failure to properly assess student learning. Strib 9-13-19

"That's the criteria." KARE 11 6-11-19
Should be criterion.

Hurray!
"Yale psychiatrist explains why Trump's aborted Iran attack is
a 'mental health issue': He 'failed every criterion [**criteria**] of
a basic mental capacity evaluation." Tana Ganeva/Raw Story
June 24, 2019

Bacteria/Bacterium — Bacteria = plural; Bacterium = singular

"The bacteria is [**are**] ..." Ch 4 7-4-19

"There was [**were**] no bacteria." Rachel Maddow 7-1-19

"E-coli bacteria is [**are**] to blame ..." both from NBC News
6-29-19

"This bacteria [**bacterium**] ..."

Julie Nelson KARE 11 6-13-19

"A rare but deadly bacteria [**bacterium**]." Lester Holt NBC News 7-1-19

Between you and I

A preposition such as *between* should be followed by an objective pronoun (such as *me, him, her, and us*) rather than a subjective pronoun (such as *I, he, she, and we*). I read somewhere that "Technically, it should be 'between you and me.' However, the phrase 'between you and I' has become accepted as an idiom of its own. Even Shakespeare used it!" So that makes it right? I don't think so.

Between two things/Among three or more

"Between [**among**] trunk highways, country roads, city roads and bridges." WCCO-TV 5-1-19

"Things weren't going especially well between [**among**] the seven Israeli, Palestinian and American teens hanging from cables …" Strib 7-27-19

Begging the question

"His answer begs a couple of questions …" Strib 12-3-08

"When redoubtable Virginia Madsen can be seen doing TV spots … it begs the question: What has happened to this Oscar nominee's career?" Strib 10-14-08

"Our search also begs the question what is the unhappiest country?" ABC 20/20 Show 1-11-08

"… her code begs a deeper question." Mensa Bulletin Jan. 2008 Letter to Editor

What does it mean to "beg the question?"

"Begs the question" does not mean something leads to a question. If something leads you to ask a question, it would be better to say, "that leads to the question," or "that invites the question."

"Begging the question" is a form of logical fallacy in which an argument is assumed to be true without evidence other than the argument itself. When one begs the question, the initial assumption of a statement is treated as already proven without any logic to show why the statement is true in the first place. (http://begthequestion.info)

The following argument begs the question.

Abortion is the unjustified killing of a human being and as such is murder. Murder is illegal. So abortion should be illegal.

The conclusion of the argument is entailed in its premises. If one assumes that abortion is murder then it follows that abortion should be illegal because murder is illegal. Thus, the arguer is assuming abortion should be illegal (the conclusion) by assuming that it is murder. In this argument, the arguer should not be granted the assumption that abortion is murder, but should be made to provide support for this claim. (Source: http://skepdic.com/begging.html)

Useless prepositions

"Omar would meet up with David Gilbert-Pederson ..." WaPo 7-8-19

<u>All Unk:</u>
Starting up the tradition.
Seek out the answer.

All the soldiers were killed off.
Where did you buy that at?
Where did you get that from?
He fell off of the roof.
Polished up.
Print out.
Headed up.

Acronyms

Lately, almost any group of initials is called an acronym. If you can pronounce it (NATO) it's an acronym. If you can't (USFWS), it isn't. It's an initialism. See how simple that was?

Stuff I hate

That being said—Thank you. I'm so stupid I didn't know it had been said. Maybe you could just say *and* or *but.*

Reach out—Too graphic for me. What's wrong with *contact*?

It is what it is—What else would it be? Defies logic.

Most instead of almost—Frequent in ON. "… one that most every waterfowler has probably seen." ON MN 11-9-18

"… something to interest most everyone." Consumer Reports May 2019

Impact—See **"More than 10 Most Common Errors—Now**

Hopefully—Yes, I know, I and many others have lost this battle and it should be in the rubble of **Examples: Myths, Battles We've Lost,** but it irritates me so much it earns a spot here.

AHD says: Nevertheless, it is clear that use of **hopefully** has become a shibboleth of 'correctness' in the language—even if the arguments on which this is based are not particularly strong—and it is wise to be aware of this in formal contexts.

Clichés—Nice parody by Joseph Epstein (Dec. 13, 2017 WSJ): About this much, surely, we can all agree: At the end of the day, given that life is a journey, and considering everything that each of us brings to the table, at a minimum we need a level playing field going forward.

Emojis—Many of the following examples came from ON. As explained earlier, I either didn't save the writer's name or I don't want to reveal the names of the writers.

Stating the obvious

"… will take effect April 30, 2005, next year …"

[Yes, that would be next year. Ran in 2004 issue.]

"… make their first cast about 9 a.m. or so in the morning."
[Yes, 9 a.m. would be in the morning.]

"Opening morning we were out at the site at 7:45 a.m."
[Yes, 7:45 a.m. would be in the morning.]

"Since it was only 3 p.m. in the afternoon ..."
[Yes, 3:30 p.m. would be in the afternoon.]

Did two different people do the writing?

Headline: "At Age 96, Backkus man is still hunting"
Photo caption: LeRoy Tilbury, 97, the oldest licensed deer hunter … What a difference a year makes.

Has the ability—I think this phraseology started with TV shopping networks. Suddenly, everything had the ability to do something.

> "They were wearing the same clothes they were captured in with no ability to wash them ..." Strib 6-24-19
> [They had the ability, not the means.]

> "These insurance companies have the ability to give you prices" WCCO Radio 11-12-18
> [Why not "... can give you prices"?]

Waiting on

> "... but said investigators are still waiting on some forensic evidence ..." Strib 4-13-19

A waiter *waits on* tables. But a dinner partner does not *wait on* you to arrive. That is the distinction that critics made for more than a century: they objected to *wait on* in the sense of *await* or *wait for*—e.g.: "They *waited on* [read *waited for*] the jury's verdict."

Even if this is not the best phrasing, however, *wait on* is now so common as a *casualism* that it can't be labeled incorrect. GMAU

Stuff that drives me nuts because 1) I still don't understand it, 2) I still have to look it up, 3) it still confuses me. (We all have our weaknesses.)

> **Commas**—Fifty percent of the time I delete them where I shouldn't. Fifty percent of the time I insert them where I shouldn't.

> The most commonly cited example of where an Oxford comma works, and how comma use, or misuse, can affect the meaning of a sentence:

> "My father the Pope and Mother Teresa."

At a very young age I heard this example: "Let's eat grandma I'm hungry."

Good, old reliable Garfield. He got the comma right: "Eat healthy, people." 5-4-19

The misplacement of commas is more than jarring, it can be costly. Excerpts from a story by Daniel Victor in the February 9, 2018 issue of The New York Times under the headline "Oxford Comma Dispute Is Settled as Maine Drivers Get $5 Million":

Ending a case that electrified punctuation pedants, grammar goons and comma connoisseurs, Oakhurst Dairy settled an overtime dispute with its drivers that hinged entirely on the lack of an Oxford comma in state law …

The dairy company in Portland, Me., agreed to pay $5 million to the drivers, according to court documents filed on Thursday …

The relatively small-scale dispute gained international notoriety last year when the United States Court of Appeals for the First Circuit ruled that the missing comma created enough uncertainty to side with the drivers, granting those who love the Oxford comma a chance to run a victory lap across the internet …

The case began in 2014, when three truck drivers sued the dairy for what they said was four years' worth of overtime pay they had been denied. Maine law requires time-and-a-half pay for each hour worked after 40 hours, but it carved out exemptions for:

The canning, processing, preserving, freezing, drying, marketing, storing, packing for shipment or distribution of:

(1) Agricultural produce;

(2) Meat and fish products; and

(3) Perishable foods.

What followed the last comma in the first sentence was the crux of the matter: "packing for shipment or distribution of." The court ruled that it was not clear whether the law exempted the distribution of the three categories that followed, or if it exempted packing for the shipment or distribution of them …

Had there been a comma after "shipment," the meaning would have been clear. David G. Webbert, a lawyer who represented the drivers, stated it plainly in an interview in March: "That comma would have sunk our ship."

Compare to compare with—Use compare to when referring to resemblance between unlike things. Use compare with for like things.

Comprise, compose—Comprise—to include. Compose—to put together, to form. Technically, comprise **can** mean *make up* or *form.* The most common abuse is the construction *comprised of.*

Passive voice—Choose active. "Bonds hits homer," not "Homer hit by Bonds."

Flat adverbs—Ever heard of a flat adverb? I hadn't until about a month ago. Seems I never should have wasted my time and that of my editor at ON correcting *deep* to *deeply.* In hundreds of columns, our writers would write something like, "He fished deep in the water column." I would change it to *deeply.* Wrong. I discovered a category of adverbs called flat adverbs.

A flat or bare adverb, is an adverb that has the same form as a related adjective and does not end in *-ly*, e.g. "drive slow," "drive fast." It's also sometimes called simple adverb.

Numbers—General rule: Spell out numbers below 10. But there are many exceptions that I have to look up every time I use a number.

Hyphens—The hyphen is the first cousin to the comma. If you read the section on "Two Words to One," you'll see but a few of the hundreds of words that have changed (see, didn't use transitioned, a very overused word) from two words to one, as *overused* has. Most of these words went from two separate words, to two words hyphenated to one word. See the evil and hard to anticipate use of hyphens? The AP declares: Hyphens are joiners. Use them to avoid ambiguity or to form a single idea from two or more words.

Examples: Hyphens needed

"3Day Sale at Slumberland" TV commercial Ch 4 11-7-18 [I'd like to buy two Saturdays and a Sunday.]

"Fat free milk." On milk carton at Byerley's supermarket. [Fat milk that's free?]

"Cage free eggs." On label of Hellman's Mayonaise. [Free eggs that are in cages, or should I be caging the free eggs?]

While there are many rules that govern hyphenation, most of them have plenty of exceptions, and some sources recommend adding hyphens to compound phrases any time it would minimize confusion. Still, there are some set phrases and other situations where hyphens are always necessary.

Passive voice – Passive voice—What's the big deal? It doesn't bother me, and I'll bet most readers of most publications don't notice it. However, my hero Bryan Garner says:

What's the real problem with using passive voice? There are three. First, passive voice usually adds a couple of unnecessary words. Second, when it doesn't add those extra words, it fails to say squarely who has done what. That is, the sentence won't mention the actor with a *by*-phrase (*The book was written* vs. *The book was written by Asimov*). Third, the passive subverts the normal word order for an English sentence, making it harder for readers to process the information. To put it a little more dramatically, "The impersonal passive voice [is] an opiate that cancels responsibility, hides identity, and numbs the reader." Sheridan Baker, "Scholarly Style, or the Lack Thereof" (1956), in *Perspectives on Style* 64, 66 (Frederick Candelaria ed., 1968).

The active voice has palpable advantages in most contexts: it saves words, says directly who has done what, and meets the reader's expectation of a normal actor–verb–object sentence order.

So maybe I'll have to change my mind.

Stuff that makes me angry

I get angry when I hear or read obvious mistakes from people who should know better, i.e., professional writers and broadcasters.

"Indeed, most of the people on Trump's list of potential Supreme Court picks, who [**whom**] he might still nominate if he gets to choose a third justice." WaPo 11-15-18

"… the amount [**number**] of people in the room." Rachel 7-9-19

"With I and the president … [**with the president and me…**] CNN chief media correspondent and host of "Media Buzz" Brian Stelter 11-11-18

"… for alternate [**alternative**] housing …" Ask Amy 6-29-19

"Controversy among [**between**] two people …" 4-14-19
KARE 11 News anchor Randy Shaver:

"Summer has arrived" because the temperature hit 90 degrees. No, summer hasn't arrived any more than spring was late this year. They're both at the same time every year.

Rachel Maddow, host of the MSNBC show of the same name (eponymous) Rhodes Scholar and Maddow holds a doctorate in politics from Oxford University.

"Me and the whole staff here …" 10-9-18
"That me and my office wrote." 5-1-19
"It's her that's the problem." 5-1-19
"There was no bacteria." Rachel Maddow 7-1-19

It's probably not fair to expect political parties to be mindful of the rules of grammar. They are more concerned about other things, and after all, it won't affect how I vote. But I somehow expect better of them.

"We're up against Democrats and interest groups that sometimes are far better funded than us [**we are**]." MN GOP

But I do think it's reasonable to expect better grammar from those who hope to do business with me.

Examples from a letter from a company seeking to manage our building:

"With that, Lorie proceeded to find a replacement, obtain her license and started [**start**] …" [Parallel construction.]

"I won't go in to [**into**] all of my background as [**because**] you are familiar with it."

"Currently 11 properties receive full-service management and 3 [**three**] receive accounting [-] only services."

"We are a small company, [delete comma] which [**that**] allows us to custom[**ize**] our services."

"It is for that reason why [**that**] our company and it's [**its**] culture reflects [**reflect**] our values."

Stuff I love

Bill Farmer

Bill Farmer was a columnist for the *St. Paul Pioneer Press* for 25 years, and a radio personality on WCCO's "Top of the Morning Show." He had a unique way of making ordinary people and everyday events interesting and whimsical. Here are examples from some of his columns.

New word

President Nixon has proposed a $5 billion budget surplus. The government still is looking up the meaning of that last word.

Do, re, who?

Now it's Mrs. Rosemary Brown.

Life Magazine has a story about a woman by that name who lives in a suburb of London. She hears regularly from Ludwig van Beethoven, Johann Sebastian Bach, Franz Liszt, Sergei Rachmaninoff and Freddy Chopin, among others.

Not only that, these characters are sending her some more music from their genius and she's writing it down and performing it. That's her bag. I'm surprised at Life Mag for swallowing so much of it.

"Debussy (sic)," says Mrs. Brown, "is a real comic. He wears the most extraordinary clothes, sometimes a sheepskin coat and straw hat. …"

I'd like to know who is in charge of the wardrobe for these spirts from the Other Side. I don't question the lady's sincerity, but it would seem to me that a spirit might more naturally flit around the cosmos as nekkid as a jaybird. After all, who's watching? It's news to me that sheepskin coats and straw hats are in the transcendental clothes closet of the Hereafter.

Eternal flame

"You have spaghetti in your water heater."

"An angel-hair vermicelli, actually," I corrected. You have to deal sternly with these artisans. He, after all, had assumed a rather affrontive and accusatory tone.

"Might I ask why?" he persisted with an unwelcomed familiarity.

"You may not. Just fix the damned thing and be gone with you." I sniffed with a wave of the hand.

In these straitened times, I had elected to do the repairs myself rather than summon a plumber, who, at hourly rates, would have the work ethic of a three-toed sloth.

The water heater has but one function and that is to heat water. When it fails in that, I am not the type of bloke who avoids immediate action, because if I did, my wife would kill me.

What can I say? She has a penchant for fast cars and hot water.

My effort at the simple repair, not unlike rewiring a nuclear submarine, resulted in the pilot light going out. Due to the nature of things, the pilot light on a water heater is about as accessible as the Taliban caves of western Pakistan.

"But it stands to reason," my reason explained to me. "The pilot must be located, by necessity and maximum efficiency directly beneath the gas burner, which, in turn, must position itself centrally beneath the tank of water that is to be heated."

The manufacturer, notorious for his several failed suicide attempts, has provided an opening for lighting the pilot that is roughly the circumference of a grape while the designated target is a foot away. It might as well be in Falkland Islands, so far as a human hand holding a lighted paper match is concerned. And if you're ever in the need of fresh air, simply stick your nose into a water heater, for there is, miraculously, always a stiffish enough breeze there to blow out an acetylene torch, let alone a matchbookful of matches.

"I can't get the infernal thing lit. It's too far from the opening." I was damned if I was going to roll up a piece of newspaper into a makeshift torch that would be guaranteed to burn down the house and much of the adjacent neighborhood.

My wife knows the warning signs. Carpet strewn with K-Mart-quality tools, beads of forehead sweat glistening in newly-formed furrows. An eye perusing the liquor cabinet.

"Try a piece of spaghetti," she said, not looking up from her latest issue of Manic Handicrafts Magazine.

"Spaghetti?"

"Yes. It will burn just like a candle and you can reach in with that."

"Where did you hear that?"

"Martha Stewart. Try it. It works."

Ordinarily I don't take advice from ex-cons, but Martha, I must say, knows her pyrotechnic pastas. Admittedly, we were out of spaghetti as we know it. There was a passable linguini that I test-fired and it produced a stable, if somewhat flattened, flame. We had a macaroni that I surmised might work if I ever needed to light something around a corner. The lasagna sheaf was out of the question—I'd save that idea in case I ever took up arson as a hobby.

No, the frail, delicate wisp of an angel-hair vermicelli would have to do. A test-lighting over the sink produced the desired result: A reliable quarter-inch flame.

I knelt by the water heater as if in prayer. Actually, I was in prayer; I always am when igniting pilot lights, or, rather, attempting to.

The explosion wasn't nearly as dramatic as those you see in the Itchy & Scratchy cartoons.

A mere ball of blue flame the size of nectarine. A scream, of course. But the face wasn't blackened the way Tom's is after Jeremiah proffers an stick of dynamite in lieu of a cigar.

And the eyelashes will grow back in a matter of weeks rather than months.

After shutting off the gas, cursing, and stepping on the business end of an errant claw hammer, I called the plumber.

Of course, he belongs to an obscure sect that forbids work of any kind for eight of the holiest months of the year. We were in month No. 3, a rather slow time, and he would be willing to break his vow of Sublime Idleness or Shpitspahtakl, for a friendly $375, plus mileage and parts.

Sent to my wife, Susan, and me while we were vacationing in Southern California:

Dear Webbers

Oh, I can see it now...Fred dressed in checkered knickerbockers, argyle stockings to the knees, plum cravat and matching beret; Susan in her satin floor-lengthed gown, feather boa, and heart-shaped sunglasses, puffing languorously on a foot-long, ivory cigarette-holder through pouting red lips, the two of you cruising along Sunset Boulevard in your cream-colored, 16-cyclindered Duesenberg toward crisscrossing searchlights that lead to admiring throngs awaiting their arrival at some motion picture premiere of their latest celluloid triumph.

Meanwhile, the overalled Farmer and his flour-sack-clad, bent-backed wife, Ol' Peg, gnaw on a straw and a corncob pipe, respectively, casting hollow stares at a cloudless sky that offers no respite for their parched and cracked plot of red clay.

Oh, the injustice of it all.

Well, you two madcaps had better start combing the confetti out of your hair because you are coming back to Reality all too soon. In the meantime, enjoy yourselves. Nibble some caviar, snort a few last grains of cocaine, spit on an illegal immigrant or two ... gad, how I miss all that!

How I miss Bill.

Dan Neil

Dan Neil is the author of the "Rumble Seat" column which runs Saturdays in *The Wall Street Journal*. Who would believe a person would look forward to the writing style of an auto reviewer?

The Gladiator shares all of the Wrangler's charms—a fold-down windshield, fully removable top, 11-inch ground clearance—and many of its flaws: the indefensible, couldn't-be-bothered fuel economy (19 mpg, combined); the painfully under-designed folding canopy top, plagiarized from a Ford Model T; and various corner-cutting that produced, in one case, a literal cut corner. Note how the Gladiator's rear doors are truncated at the lower aft? That's because they used the same door stamping as the four-door Wrangler. A penny saved is a penny earned. Such critiques are fleas on an elephant. 4-11-19

A fully loaded Gladiator Rubicon will soar into and out of the $50s,

The test drive also included a righteous overland course taking in slick axle-deep mud and bottom-banging descents down rock ravines. The Rubicons we were driving chewed this scenery like contented cows.

Jason Gay

And to double my enjoyment of reading *The Wall Street Journal* for writing style, here's an example from the Journal's sports columnist

Monday's men's college championship between Virginia and Texas Tech was widely predicted to be a duck: a snoozy, asleep-on-the couch-by-10 p.m. bore, thanks to two torpid, defense-first, low-scoring outfits certain to batter each other into somnolent submission. 4-10-19

In the lead-up, a headline on Yahoo excoriated the matchup as "generationally unsexy"—a ruthless slag that sounded like the title of a discarded Prince single.

The New Yorker

Too many examples of what I enjoy to list here! Read any article in any issue.

La Velle E. Neal III, Strib

It was a bad sign for the Mets ace, whose slider wasn't missing bats like it normally does.

Old radio programs

Radio has rightly been tagged "Theater of the Mind." Without images, it had an obligation to describe where, what, who, and when and much more. Not such an apt description lately because AM radio programming has evolved into sports or talk. But back in the day ...

"She wore a dress that fit like lacquer on a Chinese vase." [Sam Spade Circ. 1950.]

"You look like you just shot six hole in the high 80s."

Rocky Fortune "Shipboard Jewel Robbery" [1953

Starring Frank Sinatra]

"Crazy like King Solomon."

"As sad as the word 'Mother' in an orphanage. [Pat Novak for Hire—1950s]

"Rain smelled like a wet used blanket at a fire sale."

"I walked away from him like he had smallpox and I'd never been vaccinated."

"He was bouncing around inside the car like the ball in a handball court." [Michael Shane describing a man in a car tumbling down a cliff.]

"As quiet as a washing machine filled with pennies." [Pat Novak for Hire.]

"Disappeared like a fart in the wind on the Ponderosa." [Billions 6-3-18. Sorry, couldn't resist. It's from a current TV program]

"Making more noise than a venetian blind in a typhon." [Pat Novak]

"As cold as a can of beans." [Jeff Regan]

Writers Morton Fine and David Friedkin had a special ability to evoke images of Manhattan in the radio show "Broadway is my Beat (CBS 1949-1954). The show opened with lead character, Lt. Danny Clover, intoning, "Broadway is my beat. The gaudiest, most violent, lonesomest mile in the world." Here are excerpts from two shows:

When night comes to Broadway, it drains through neon before it scatters the streets and everywhere shadows are tinged with scarlet, and a crowd gathers, the tribe of Twilight till Dawn. The roar that coils upon itself before it floods the darkness.

Lean against it. Walk it. The whirlpool of mob. The puffs of music from waking doorways. The swirl of women's laughter that passes your lips. Let it touch you. Then look backwards see it all change in the night wind and drift away.

Broadway, where the measured screaming of the spectaculars [large, lighted outdoor ads] echoes into the wilderness of the night. And their cadence is the beat of a metallic and mechanical heart. This is the rhythm of the life you're assigned to on Broadway. There's nothing you can do about it. Your challenge is with a whisper, or a plea or a cry and there's no one to hear it because Broadway's ears are tuned only to throb of a mechanical heart. Broadway, my beat.

Dennis Anderson

Anderson is a sports columnist for the Strib. Pretty classy stuff for the sports section:

> From a distance, the structure's lighted, open sides lent it a spaceship's diffused glow.

From his column about Father's Day:

> A bit of an outlier to his in-laws, Dad was a fisherman, and a Camel-smoking fisherman at that. Come Sundays, he was in the proper pew listening to Grandpa preach. But his more universalist beliefs pivoted on the special kind of salvation a live minnow impaled on a small hook can deliver, and he tested that faith whenever possible.

Fun stuff

Richard Lederer, in the July 2019 issue of the Mensa Bulletin, points out that Noah Webster (1758-1843) included in his dictionaries new American words, among them *applesauce, bullfrog chowder, handy, hickory, succotash, tomahawk* and *skunk*: "a quadruped remarkable for its smell."

Webster also was responsible for deleting the *u* from words like *honour* and *labour*, and the *k* from the likes of *musick* and *publick*. He also reversed the last two letters in words such as *centre* and *theatre*.

The following grammar jokes, if that's what they are, are all over the internet and my efforts to find an author have failed. They sound like the kinds of statements (not jokes?) Stephen Wright would make.

A dangling participle walks into a bar. Enjoying a cocktail and chatting with the bartender, the evening passes pleasantly.

A bar was walked into by the passive voice.

An oxymoron walked into a bar, and the silence was deafening.

A malapropism walks into a bar, looking for all intensive purposes like a wolf in cheap clothing, muttering epitaphs and casting dispersions on his magnificent other, who takes him for granite.

Hyperbole totally rips into this insane bar and absolutely destroys everything.

A non sequitur walks into a bar. In a strong wind, even turkeys can fly.

A comma splice walks into a bar, it has a drink and then leaves.

At the end of the day, a cliché walks into a bar — fresh as a daisy, cute as a button, and sharp as a tack.

The subjunctive would have walked into a bar, had it only known.

A misplaced modifier walks into a bar owned a man with a glass eye named Ralph.

A simile walks into a bar, as parched as a desert.

A gerund and an infinitive walk into a bar, drinking to forget.

Proofreading tips

There are many, many, many proofreading tips on the internet. Some seem to be directed at proofing scholarly dissertations, some for technical journals, and some I don't even understand. Sticking with my Preface remark that this is not meant to be a thorough, comprehensive grammar guide, I will provide those I think are most practical for my purposes and, I hope, yours.

> Find the time to do it. Pay attention to deadlines, but find adequate time and some place where there are no distractions if possible.

> Read from a printed copy, not a computer screen or monitor.

> Read aloud what you wrote. Does it make sense? You'll also run across errors you'll want to correct. To not lose the sense of what I'm reading, I usually just put a red check mark in the margin to remind me go back to those areas.

> Then read it for spelling, grammar, syntax, usage, subject-verb agreement, and all the other stuff (modifier placement,

pronoun agreement, I've written about! DO NOT TRUST SPELL CHECKING FEATURES.

Double check any math.

If you have time, read aloud it again!

Read books and style manuals. A number of them have been given throughout these chapters.

Conclusions

Learn to accept change.

Judge not lest ye also be judged.

I thought I knew it all, but I didn't. You don't either.

Words are fun, interesting and instructive. Enjoy them.

Grammar, syntax, usage, etc., are matters of style. Keep up to changes.

Best way to learn is to read.

The greatest danger in writing about grammar, usage, style, etc., is making mistakes. And I have. In the beginning, I tried to joke that I made mistakes "to see if you could catch them." Super-lame, I know. Grammar Vultures are perched on the power lines outside my office and home, waiting to pick at my grammatical bones. And that's OK. I'd do the same. If you do have questions or comments, I'm not including contact information for obvious reasons, but you can forward them to the publisher.

"That hastily-written contributions to journals contain errors in grammar, and are faulty in construction, is not to be wondered at; but that there should be, in treatises on those errors, the identical faults which those treatises are written to condemn, is a circumstance well calculated to impress all students of the language, with the necessity for increased vigilance; for, if those who have specially devoted their time to the cultivation of a pure and accurate style of writing, occasionally fail to write correctly, even after their most careful efforts, how numerous must be the faults of those who consider that but little attention on their part is needed, to perfect themselves in the knowledge and use of their mother tongue."—**George Washington Moon** 1823 – 1909

APPENDIX A

Think Piece
By Robert M. Shaw, MNA Manager Emeritus March 10, 2009

A better way, perhaps, to own a newspaper.

I learned two hard lessons about newspapers when I was a young fellow running the *Othello Outlook*, a small weekly in eastern Washington State.

1. Everything in the newspaper business depends on advertising.
2. News—that is to say, journalism—is expensive.

My newspaper's future, the future of my five employees, and my own future every day hung by a single thread: a full-page grocery ad from Ed Emry's IGA Market up on the hill. For two years, if Ed ever decided to pull his ad I wouldn't have been able to meet my payroll. I would have had to fold the paper, fire my Linotype operator and one printer, and try to eke out a living from commercial printing.

We always, therefore, handled Ed's account with great respect. I picked up the ad copy myself, and when it was set I proofed it ver-r-ry carefully. He always saw a page proof. My four employees were well aware of the danger we were in. We all bought our groceries from Ed. I suggested that when we shopped at his store we *let him know* we were there. There was another grocery store in town, and I kept trying—and failing—to get the owner to advertise with me. He was very happy with fliers which, he claimed, cost much less than advertising in my paper.

So from week to week Ed Emry held my newspaper in the palm of one hand. I am happy to say that we survived. Industry eventually came to town with more subscribers, more businesses, more money. That first year, though, was a very close call. More than once I thought: "This is one hell of a way to own a newspaper."

My second lesson was what it cost to publish the news. I came from the news-side, but until I was responsible for the whole operation I never fully realized that news is expensive.

Publishing news in my town chiefly meant gathering and publishing facts about local government: city council, school board, police, and to some extent county. School and city boards met Monday nights. I liked to use quotes in my stories. Many long evenings I sat a on a little plastic chair, made notes, went to the office, tried to read my notes, and wrote a late-night story so that Old John, my Linotype operator, would have something to set the next morning when he came to work, bitching and complaining every foot of the way.

I could tell from certain comments that people liked my coverage of local government. They liked those quotes. We noticed new subscribers coming in.

But this gathering and publishing facts took a lot of time and attention. It meant trying to tell what actually was going on behind the scenes at city hall and in the schools. It meant catching hell for spelling "Olson" instead of "Olsen." It meant facing a local lawyer who threatened to sue me for libel. It meant editing copy from barely literate "country correspondents."

Everything in the newspaper business depends on advertising. News—that is to say, journalism—is expensive.

My newspaper's future, the future of my five employees, and my own future every day hung by a thread.

Other aspects of the job were easy. I actually enjoyed getting out and making the "ad rounds." Feeding the press or folder every Wednesday was *fun.* I even got satisfaction from going out to collect past-due accounts which I had inherited. But digging out those stubborn facts—and getting them right—was hard, demanding, and expensive work. But it was the news that made everything else worth-while.

There must be a better way to own a newspaper. I say this, of course, as—incredibly—we watch our state's leading newspaper, the *Minneapolis Star and Tribune*, struggling in bankruptcy. Ideas about better "economic models" are floating around. One possible model, some say, is the non-profit corporation. Public radio does a very good job with news. Why can't a newspaper?

What's wrong with it, I say, is that it puts journalism right back under the thumb of government. Non-profit corporations may not engage in political activity—they may not, for example, endorse a candidate. We should remember that several years ago conservative members of the F.C.C. put real pressure on NPR editors to cover the news more to their liking.

The co-operative model, in which customers own the company and share in the profits, seems better. There are a lot of them in Minnesota, about 700, and they successfully function in many different fields: finance (credit unions), utilities (REA, telephone, cable), consumer coops (Health Partners, Cenex), producer coops (ethanol, Land O'Lakes), worker coops, mutual insurance, and news (the Associated Press).

We have a member-owned newspaper in Minnesota, a weekly, the *Farmers Independent*, in Bagley. Another exists in Frederic, Wisconsin, the *Inter-County Leader*.

Tom Burford, editor of the *Farmers Independent*, says his newspaper was established as a co-op in 1918 and there has never been a challenge to its ownership. Shares are restricted. No person can buy more than ten shares (which are currently paying 8 percent) and may not sell them. An elected board serves as publisher. Tom has served as editor since 1991. "The board has have never meddled with content," Tom says. "They may make suggestions, but not orders. They just want me to put out a good newspaper."

I discussed this with a friend, a newspaperman. "Oh sure!" he said. "A local board sitting there as publisher! They'd meddle, all right."

That could happen, I responded, but what would you rather have as publisher? Local people or some financier sitting 2,000 miles away?

For years I believed that family ownership was the best way to own a newspaper. That tradition is a thing of the past. I can count only 12 Minnesota newspapers owned and operated by sons or daughters of publishers.

There must be a better way. The cooperative deserves a closer look. – RMS

Permission is given to reprint this Think Piece

APPENDIX B

Wördos Quiz
2006 Minnesota Newspaper Convention

Circle or write in the correct choice or answer.

1. **I walk (everyday/every day) that I can.**
2. **Which of these is the correct spelling?**

   *** ocassion**
   *** occasion.**
   *** occassion.**

3. **James Smith was elected to the city council with a (majority/ plurality) of the votes cast. Smith had 43 percent of the votes cast, Jones had 38 percent and Johnson had 19 percent.**
4. **Place apostrophes in the correct places.**

   Thursdays classes were cancelled because of Professor Jones illness so the students met in the womens lounge.

5. **Half of the tools (that/which) Tom used were new.**
6. **He said it would be (alright/all right) if we stayed the night.**

7. **Eight senators proposed a bill Wednesday to push the use of (alternate/alternative) fuels.**

8. **The average temperature in Minneapolis in January is 13.1 degrees, (compared to/compared with) San Diego, where the average temperature is 57.8 degrees.**

9. **The dog (lay/laid/lain) silently on the chair for two days before his owner noticed him.**

10. **Send a memo to keep them (appraised/apprised) of the results of the tests.**

Answers to 2006 MNA Quiz

1. *Every day* is correct. As two words, it's an adverb. As one word, *everyday* is an adjective meaning *used daily* or *common*, as in "Those are his everyday shoes. He wears them every day."

2. *Occasion* is correct.

3. *Plurality* is correct. It means the most votes received, but fewer than half. *Majority* means more than half.

4. Thursday's, Jones' (AP Stylebook: use only an apostrophe for forming possessive of singular proper names ending in *s*), women's.

5. *That* is correct. *Which* introduces clauses that are not essential to a sentence (and, generally, *which* clauses must be set off by commas). *That* clauses are essential to understanding the meaning (here, we're talking about Tom's tools, and no one else's).

6. *All right* is always correct. It is always two words. There is no *alright*.

7. *Alternative* is correct—a choice between two or more things. *Alternate*—happening or following in turns.

8. *Compared with* is correct. You *compare with* to point out a difference. You *compare to* to show similarity.

9. *Lay* is correct. It is the past tense of *lie*, an intransitive verb meaning to recline or be situated. *Lain* is the past participle of

lie (lie, lay, lain). *Laid* is an altogether different word. It is the past tense of the *lay* that is the action verb meaning to put or to place.

10. *Apprised* is correct. It means to inform. *Appraise* means to determine the value of something.